Praise for

OUR FRIENDLY LOCAL TERRORIST

To label anyone a terrorist is fraught with emotion and politics; all the more since September 11th. And far too often the label is misplaced and unfounded. Mary Jo Leddy's important book powerfully reminds us that the mistakes, secrecy, and lack of accountability for calling anyone a terrorist can be a devastating source of injustice.

— ALEX NEVE, Secretary General, Amnesty International Canada (English branch)

In this honest, important book, Mary Jo Leddy reminds us that injustice thrives when citizens do not use their voices. Individuals can make a difference. Even in Canada justice is not the result of an easy, natural process. It is up to all Canadians who love their country to change the status quo for the better. Every Canadian should read this book.

— MARINA NEMAT, author of *Prisoner of Tehran*

Our Friendly Local Terrorist is a work of deep and searching compassion. It is proof once again that the pen is far mightier than the sword and that truths will wend their way to us no matter how dense and oppressive the systems that cage and deny them.

— JOY KOGAWA, author of *Obasan*

A chilling story that shakes your faith in our vaunted Canadian immigration system. Secret hearings, spying, betrayal, no accountability are features we associate with desperate dictatorships elsewhere, not our own government here in Canada.

It is no wonder Canada's stature in the human rights world has sunk to its lowest level ever. This is a national disgrace.

— HELGA STEPHENSON, human rights activist

MARY JO LEDDY

OUR FRIENDLY LOCAL

TERRORIST

BETWEEN THE LINES

TORONTO

First published in 2010 by
Between the Lines
720 Bathurst Street, Suite #404
Toronto, Ontario M5S 2R4
Canada
1-800-718-7201
www.btlbooks.com

Library and Archives Canada Cataloguing in Publication

Leddy, Mary Jo, 1946–
    Our friendly local terrorist / Mary Jo Leddy.

ISBN 978-1-897071-60-1

1. Goven, Suleyman. 2. Refugees, Kurdish—Canada—Biography.
3. Refugees, Kurdish—Turkey—Biography. 4. Canadian Security
Intelligence Service. 5. Kurds—Canada—Biography. I. Title.

FC3097.26.G69L43 2010   325'.21092   C2010-901027-2

Cover and text design: Gordon Robertson
Cover images: Security camera by Gautier Willaume/iStockphoto;
    people by Giorgio Fochesato/iStockphoto; Suleyman Goven by Mary Jo Leddy

Printed in Canada

Between the Lines gratefully acknowledges assistance for its publishing
activities from the Canada Council for the Arts, the Ontario Arts Council,
the Government of Ontario through the Ontario Book Publishers Tax Credit
program and through the Ontario Book Initiative, and the Government of
Canada through the Canada Book Fund.

In memory of

Seyit Riza

and the 70,000 victims
of the Dersim massacre 1937–38

Seyit Riza, the leader of the Dersim region,
was a relative of Suleyman Goven.

The official history of Turkey long claimed that
the government had taken necessary measures
to quell the rebellion of Kurdish "terrorists."
More recently a few government officials
acknowledged the "massacre" of Dersim.

He was left alone.
And he struggled
all night, until the break of day.

When the faceless one saw
that winning was not possible,
he was wounded and left limping.

The nameless one said
Let me go
but he said
I will not let you go
until you bless me.

— an adaptation of GENESIS 32:24–27

CONTENTS

1

A T LEAST AN OCEAN of difference separates the Prairie town of my childhood from the rugged mountains of eastern Turkey where Suleyman Goven grew up.

And a vast indifference.

It is not only a difference of perspective, although it is that too. Even the most scenic mountains overwhelm me after a while. They loom in my mind. As Suleyman Goven has loomed and lingered in my mind for almost two decades.

I am more comfortable with a long and liquid horizon, with the colour of lilacs and lilies blooming in the sky at night. Out there, in Saskatchewan, you can see the disappearing point and who is coming down the road.

I have never seen the mountains of eastern Turkey or the Kurdish area of Dersim, the place of massacre where suffering riffles along cold streams. But I have seen the face of Suleyman Goven, the landscape of a particular history—rugged, stubborn in its refusal to submit to the fog of secrecy and silence.

I grew up with stories of how the very earth could blow away in the wind. In spite of this, and perhaps because of it, we Prairie people became stubborn in another way, taking our bearings from the clear and consequential sky.

The Saskatoon of the 1950s where I grew up was a small town divided by the South Saskatchewan River. It was, according to anyone I knew, a very friendly place. We had a friendly local newspaper, friendly local police, and friendly local store. During the long summer days our parents would shoo us out in the morning and we would run around the neighbourhood and even beyond, certain of our safety.

Wherever the word terrorism was invented, it was not in Saskatoon, at least not as I remember it. My childhood was a time of innocence, or so I thought until I met Suleyman Goven. He had a childhood too; and he could sometimes become quite childlike again. But innocence? No, it seems that was never given to him. After I met him I began to see scars running long and deep through my own country, and I would see my Prairie river in a different light.

Suleyman Goven, like the mountains of his homeland, is both a fact and a revelation—about him and about the rest of us.

He was tagged as a terrorist.

He was accused of being one of them.

• • •

How on earth did this happen? This book is a response to that question. It is a response more than an answer because the truth is so much stranger.

This is the story of Suleyman Goven as I have gathered it up in the course of years of casual conversations, in focused interviews, and through his own diary, which he began to write as he left Turkey and began the long journey towards Canada. It has also, at least partly, become my own story.

This is not a book that I wanted to write. A sleuth might be attracted by the sad mystery that lies at the core of this story. A writer of thrillers might be intrigued by the cosmic dimensions of the struggle that surfaced at times. As a trained academic, I find very little in this material that challenges me intellectually. Nevertheless, it leaves me feeling undone as a human being. Truth can be the stranger who makes it difficult to go home.

This is a book I have been afraid to write. I put it aside for years, preferring to leave what happened to the courts and the political process. There are still moments when I doubt that the pen is mightier than the sword of secrecy. I have a box full of letters to politicians, Immigration officials, and prime ministers detailing reasons as to why Suleyman Goven needed and deserved justice.

And still he is tagged as a terrorist.

And still he resists, solid as the mountains, compact as rock: refusing to submit to the persuasion and coercion of secret services; refusing to disappear into one of the holes of oblivion opened by the cracks in bureaucracies throughout the world.

Fear stopped me from writing and fear started me writing—fear not only for Suleyman but also for myself, for my country.

There are days when an old harpy of fear presses on my shoulder and whispers: *they will smear you with him, they will never admit a mistake. Let it go.*

Yet another messenger also arrives at such times, with a pure air of purpose. *There is no other. This you must write.*

Words like Annunciation and Visitation come to mind. Yet this is not some sweet angel from the supermarket. The message burns at my fingertips. I know I am summoned, addressed, commanded. I could say no as easily as I can say yes. Life impresses, but it does not impose.

This you must do; there is no other.

．　．　．

I became a witness to Suleyman's story on a seemingly endless day in October 1994. That was the day I heard the *howl*. That was the day on which I became especially burdened with a peculiar knowledge of the difference between good and evil. I have always felt blessed by my country, but that was a day on which I felt the immense burden of something I heard and saw. This I must write, not only for Suleyman Goven but also for Canada, my home and native land.

This I must write so I can go home.

I am surprised that that these reflections, about a supposed terrorist, are so shaped by religious imagery. Perhaps it is my own need to see things in a steady way, and to see them whole. Words like pain and injustice do not reach down deep enough to the kind of spiritual bedrock you seek when you are in the grip of a great fear. Words like suffering and redemption wind their way through the centuries and up through the layers of my selves upon selves.

There are times and places, though, when religious images are more than metaphors for some inner spiritual state. In extreme situations, they become descriptions of reality. Like Jacob, Suleyman Goven has wrestled through a long night of years, not hours, with something or someone, and he has been wounded and left limping and is still seeking a blessing. He is, in the words of the prophet Isaiah, "a man of suffering and acquainted with grief."

He is no angel—unless angels swear like troopers—but he is not a demon.

When I first made the acquaintance of people called spies and terrorists, I felt as though I had entered some kind of underworld in which angels and demons were locked in a great moral struggle. Now, as in the most ancient days, that world seemed to be divided between US and THEM.

This book describes how the lines between these two worlds began to blur. The agents who were supposed to protect me and my country became more menacing as Suleyman became, for me, far less problematic. At times I felt at war within myself, unsure of who was us or who was them. Gradually I reclaimed some basic sense of reality. On the one hand, I became convinced that we demonize others because we do not want to face the ways in which rather ordinary people are capable of contributing to bitter suffering. On the other hand, I became certain that we idealize angels and set them outside ourselves because we do not want to admit that we ourselves have the power to do good in the world.

The angels and the demons are within each one of us, and we have the choice as to which of them will prevail. Depending on the stories we tell and what we choose to remember, we will add either to the goodness or to the suffering of the world.

I have determined to remain life-size in this story, and to reinstate Suleyman and his tormentors as part of the human family. To remain life-size in a time of being diminished by terror—that is the moral struggle of our era and of our world.

As you read on, you will understand why I, together with various courts and tribunals in Canada, have concluded that Suleyman is not a terrorist. This was not a hasty conclusion on their part, or on my part. There were days on which I had grave doubts about

Suleyman, about myself. What if? What if they are right? These were weighty questions. Innocent people could be involved; my own integrity was on the line.

I am also sure that Suleyman must have wondered whether he could count on me in the end. Would I be willing to risk my public reputation and integrity on some obstinate Kurdish guy?

Yes.

That is the answer. Yet the reason why I have stayed with his struggle over so many years is not so simple to explain. He is too old to be my son, and I am too young to be his mother. We could hardly be called friends; months can pass without our paths crossing. I am glad when he does not call.

Still, I know that at some point he will call, and I will respond. I think this is called loyalty, not a cool word in the throwaway culture. This is also about respect, for I have come to respect his immense complexity, his humanity. And Suleyman respects me, I know this. Even now he bows slightly when he shakes my hand.

We listen to each other, attentively even when understanding escapes us. Only once have I heard him cry. It was on a day when he was in my office, reading from his diary, and I was sitting, with my back to him, typing away intermittently as he slowly read through the pages he had written over many years. That was what we did, together, when we were pulling out the information that we needed for this book. Suleyman would translate from the Turkish, and I would "English" the sentences. On that day at one point his voice halted completely. Preparing to write this book was always something of a halting process, but this was something different.

"I walked towards the house and saw the religious men washing the body of my father in the backyard. I took his hand and bent down to kiss it . . ."

I did not turn around to try to console him. I could not enter that space. I waited and listened until Suleyman came back to here, back to now, and then he started to translate once again and I typed on, aware of the ocean of difference between us—that was no longer such a vast indifference.

HE WAS LEFT ALONE

WE LIVED in the same neighbourhood in Toronto, but it would be years before we met each other. I had gone to that city in the early 1970s to study and, like so many others, had stayed. Suleyman Goven had fled to Toronto in 1991, but in some fundamental way he has yet to arrive.

In 1991 I moved into a no-name part of Toronto, an area north of Bloor where Dundas bends west. It seemed like a good place to help relocate people who were no longer certain about who they were or what they could become. I moved in this direction as part of a group of people who wanted to create a community of welcome for refugees. The community, anchoring itself in three old houses and a storefront in the neighbourhood, was called Romero House.

It is a long way from Saskatoon to the West End of Toronto, as long as a lifetime and as lengthy as another story. Suffice it to say that, in 1991, I was teaching theology at the University of Toronto and also finding a home with refugees. I was happy at the thought of creating a space of welcome for them when they first arrived, often in a state of deep distress, ripped away from their homelands by cruel political currents or flash floods of social frenzy.

The first refugees we welcomed were mostly from the Horn of Africa. Elegant and polite, cheerful and wise, they taught me important things about hospitality and community. It was a privilege for me to live with them.

• • •

Meanwhile, below Bloor Street, a few blocks away, a young Kurdish man was limping up and down Roncesvalles Avenue looking for someone to talk to. He would barely escape becoming a permanent member of the homeless underclass that is so often talked about as an issue or a cause in the city. His name was Suleyman Goven, and he had arrived at Lester B. Pearson International Airport in the early spring of 1991.

The bare facts are these. Suleyman Goven, an Alevi Kurd, was raised in a family of peasant farmers in eastern Turkey. The Kurds—over twenty million people who live in a homeland, traditionally called Kurdistan, divided between four countries (eastern Turkey, eastern Syria, western Iran, northern Iraq)—are reputed to be "the world's largest ethnic minority without a territory of their own."[1] Suleyman Goven and his family became victims of the political bitterness and turmoil that engulfed relations between the Turkish government and minority Kurds in the twentieth century. Suleyman himself managed to be educated as a mechanical engineer, spent a short time in the Turkish army, got a well-paying and responsible job in Turkey's railway system, and in the process became something of a union activist and socialist. Because of his union activities—and partly because of his ethnicity and religion—he was more than once detained by police, jailed, and tortured. In the summer of 1990 Suleyman's father was killed by extreme leftist militants who suspected the elder Goven of collaborating with the Turks. Finally, in 1991, with his life at severe risk, Suleyman had to flee the country, making the difficult journey across Europe to Ireland and finally to Canada to seek refuge. He arrived at Pearson Airport on April 8, 1991. He was recognized as a Convention Refugee in 1993.

His first year in Canada was such a lonely time that he would often turn to writing in his diary, which he had started to keep on the day he left his country. Written in Turkish—the language in which Suleyman had done all his studies—Dear Diary became his closest and for a time his only friend. In it Suleyman would detail his daily struggle to survive or share memories that afflicted him, which often began as the pain in his feet.

The diary provides a particular insight into what it means to arrive in this country alone, without language or money, with nothing left but the desire to live. "People write in more difficult situations," he once told me. "When they are comfortable they don't write too much. When I was in jail I wrote poems."

Suleyman arrived in Toronto with $90 in his pocket. The money he had saved as a well-paid engineer in Turkey had dried up as he made his uncertain way to Canada. At Pearson Airport he presented the officers with a student visa and passed through the usual immigration procedures. During a conversation with an Immigration officer, Suleyman asked him if he knew of any Kurdish community organization in the city. The officer replied that he had no idea, had never heard of Kurds. Still, he did not wash his hands of this new arrival and went to get one of the airport workers, a Somali man named Hussein, who offered to drive Suleyman to the Jamie Mosque on Boustead Avenue, a few blocks south of Bloor off Roncesvalles.

The Imam of the mosque welcomed him, even though Suleyman was not technically a Muslim. The new arrival stayed there, sleeping on the floor, for eight days and nights. At the end of that time, without a cent left to his name, he was completely dependent on the mosque, not only for shelter but also for food.

It was Ramadan, and Suleyman felt obligated to fast and perform prayers with the others in the mosque. This practice was actually against his beliefs. As part of the minority Kurdish group called the Alevis, he had a religion that did not adhere to the Muslim practices of the dominant Sunni Kurdish groups.[2] The Sunnis make up 80 per cent of the Kurdish population in Turkey, and the Alevis only 20 per cent. The Alevis are not considered practising Muslims by the Sunnis, which has resulted in a kind of double discrimination for the Alevi Kurds and tensions between the two groups. When introduced to one of the Muslim sheiks, Suleyman refused to kiss his hand, an attitude that angered those present. Unbending as the mountains, the backbone of the earth.

After his somewhat fractious stay in the mosque, he spent several weeks moving from room to room in the same area of the city, sharing small spaces with various single Kurdish men. He was passed from person to person, moving on when he realized there was not enough food or not enough welcome. He tried desperately to get some form of government assistance, but he could find no one who would tell him how to do that. On May 21 he wrote in his diary:

It would be nice if I had my own room because I feel like I'm suffocating in this atmosphere. If you are different from them, they want to suppress you. They want to break your strength.

On the one hand I want to get some friends, and on the other hand I want to get away from them. I wake up in the middle of the night very depressed and demoralized.

Finally Suleyman figured out where the welfare office was and walked twenty blocks to get there. The social worker he met with said that he could not get assistance until he had made a refugee claim. This was something he had wanted to do from the beginning, but no one had yet taken the time to tell him exactly how to do it. The social worker gave him the address of the Immigration office in Etobicoke.

Six times he made the long walk to the Immigration office, each time barely understanding what was being asked for, each time returning home with yet another piece of paper to be filled out. The office was eight kilometres from the room he was staying in. Each time his limp became more pronounced.

He asked some of the Kurds he knew if they would drive him out to the office in Etobicoke, if they would translate for him so that he could understand what the Immigration officers were saying. They had other things to do. They were completely focused on their own survival. Suleyman had nothing to offer in return.

Eventually a face emerged in an apparently faceless system. A thoughtful Immigration officer named Margaret noticed how often Suleyman had come, how tired he seemed. She went to find a translator and someone to help him fill out the application to make a refugee claim.

"I am a Kurd from Turkey," he wrote. Thus it began.

He was lonely, but not entirely alone. Canada had long had a small number of Kurdish immigrants, but the first real wave of Kurdish refugees to the country came in 1986–87. At that time Canada still did not require visas for citizens of Turkey. The next wave of Kurdish refugees would come after the first Gulf War in 1991, around the time of Suleyman's arrival. Many Kurds from Iraq had fled to Turkey, abandoned by the United States and its allies. The Iraqi Kurds set up refugee camps in the eastern part of Turkey. This was a situation that was intolerable to the Turkish government and there were terrible reprisals against all Kurds in that area of the country. The result was a stream of refugees. By the 1990s Toronto's Kurdish population, the largest concentration in the country, was estimated at 1,400.[3]

For Suleyman, the indifference of his fellow Kurds was a shock. He decided not to associate with his own community and withdrew into himself. After he received his first social assistance cheque he paid $300 as the first month's rent for a small room on Fern Avenue, just off Roncesvalles south of Bloor. The landlady and all the other boarders in the old three-storey house were Polish. The smell of sausage and beer permeated the walls. On the advice of some of the other men living in the house, Suleyman enrolled in an English as a Second Language (ESL) class at the Polish Parishes Credit Union on Roncesvalles.

Slowly he began to piece together the makings of a habitation. That first cheque also gave him the ability to go out and buy some food and the few things that made cooking and eating possible. On Wednesday, June 5, he wrote:

Today I went shopping with $27.00. I purchased a clock and can hear the tick-tock. Even the sound of this clock is making me happy. Because I had forgotten about time. I also bought three plates and two bowls and glasses and coffee cups. I hadn't been able to cook because I didn't have anything to cook with.

So now I was able to eat boiled eggs, cheese, and olives, and fruit and tea.

Now, he told his diary, he was happy because he did not have to bother other people to get help with food.

With his next cheque he bought a pen and a cooking pot.

The nights were long, and he was alone. His English homework took several hours, and sometimes the Polish guys invited him in for a drink. Many evenings he broke out of his solitary existence and walked up and down Queen Street, the busy main street not far south of his rooming house. Walking along Queen West became his first course in Canadian social studies. He was shocked by the obvious poverty and unemployment, by the drug addicts and alcoholics, by the general sense of unhappiness he saw. Prostitutes accosted him regularly, and he was repelled by their desperate energy.

One evening, as he turned north from Queen onto Roncesvalles, he saw an open door that was casting a warm interior light onto the sidewalk. Inside people were talking quietly, and he could smell coffee brewing. Someone in the doorway motioned for him to come in, and as he did so several people standing by the entranceway shook his hand. "You are welcome. You are welcome. You are welcome." For the first time since his arrival in Canada he felt like a human being, a good person. He went further into the building and down steps into some kind of a meeting being held in what turned out to be a church basement. The people at the gathering smiled in a sad sort of way. They reminded him of people he knew from somewhere.

It was an open door that he would return to once a week or so for companionship and coffee. One of the great benefits of regularly going to these gatherings was that they provided him with the opportunity to practise his English vocabulary.

The meetings, he found, were quite formal. At the beginning of a meeting, people would stand up and introduce themselves. Eventually he found the words to stand up and say, "My name is Suleyman Goven." Everyone clapped. They would clap at almost anything he said.

After a month or two Suleyman consulted his dictionary and realized, much to his surprise, that he had been going to meetings of Alcoholics Anonymous. At the beginning of the next meeting he decided to come clean, and stood up. "My name is Suleyman Goven and I am a refugee." Everyone clapped. Then he added, "And I am not an alcoholic." Someone responded, "Don't worry Suleyman, everyone says that, everyone's in denial."

"But I'm not. It is not my . . . my . . . way."

"Sure. Sure."

He felt at home with these people, perhaps because they seemed to be in another kind of prison. When he found more words, he would tell them about the suffering of the Kurds and why so many Kurds had to leave Turkey. He kept feeling that he should be saying something else.

Now, between his attendance at these meetings and the ESL classes, he was beginning to run with the language, breathe it in and out of his mind and his mouth. At the language classes he was the only Kurd in a room full of Poles. He went to the library, borrowed tapes and books, and studied the newspapers.

Within months a goal took shape in his mind. He would go to university and become qualified to work as a mechanical engineer in Canada. Once he had a good job he could send money home to the family members he had left behind in Turkey. Maybe they could buy a house and move out of the shack they were living in. Maybe he would be able to get married sometime and have kids of his own.

• • •

Survival involves two choices: the choice not to die and the choice to live. And the choices are not the same. Suleyman had made a determined choice not to die, but the choice to live was also difficult and complicated. It is a choice he struggles with even now.

In those first months in Toronto Suleyman especially missed his family and friends, the people who knew him by name. He was cheered in mid-June when he received his first letter from his family. He wrote in his diary: "A nice letter from my brother. I was so happy. It was happiness mixed with tears. It seems like my family comes before everything. I realized this particularly after my father was killed. It is in political organizations where you collide because everyone joins for their own reasons."

There were dreams in the night, visitors from long ago and far away knocking at the door of his small room. "I dreamt of you my father last night," he wrote on July 2. "It was snowing outside and I saw you my father standing outside and I asked you to come in but you didn't say anything. You were just waiting."

Sometimes the dreams were more like anxious hopes. In one of his dreams that first year he got married, and, he wrote, "I was so excited, but I know it's not true." In Turkey he had wanted to become engaged to a young woman, Sukran, but then had been forced to leave the country. Back home he had also become infatuated with another woman, Nurhan, but she had left Turkey for Germany—he had visited her there on his journey across Europe.

He was regretful now that he had had the chance to get married in Turkey, but was not able to. He thought Sukran would have been "a perfect wife," and he was missing her. "I don't know when or who I could marry. I would like to marry someone from my community. I don't know. Time will tell."

At times the news from home was painful. Towards the end of July, picking up a newspaper from Turkey he saw a story about a young human rights lawyer who had died in an automobile accident. It was Elif Tuncer, a lawyer who had tried to defend him when he had first been arrested and tortured in Turkey. "I started to cry because she was beautiful and young and wanted to change the world," he wrote in his diary on July 29. He remembered when she had visited him in prison—a "pretty and dark-skinned lady" who was just about his own age. According to the news story, she had been arrested in March, and tortured, "not just once but several times." She was chair of the Adana branch of the Human Rights Association of Turkey and a member of the human rights commission. She and four others who died in the car crash had been on their way to participate in a funeral ceremony for the assassinated chair of the People's Democracy Party.

> I don't know how to forget this nice lady. It is hard for me to write because I am crying. I realize it is a life sentence when you lose someone you love and your life is empty and meaningless. I don't know what to do except just accept it and cry. If only I could bring her back.
>
> The bright signs of our future are disappearing one by one. Dear one, you will always be with me at the bottom of my heart. As a famous singer and writer wrote, "You will never be

forgotten." We never had a wedding ceremony for you because you were engaged in the struggle for the people. I know as a Kurdish woman you stood up against the double standard. You became a lawyer for your people. If we get our rights one day I know we will hear you when you are flying in the sky. . . . With your wings you will wave to us, and in front of you, with tears in my eyes and with my wounded heart, I will continue to live and to curse life. So long, my dear friend.

In the fall of 1991 Suleyman found an electronics course he could take at George Harvey Collegiate, a fair distance north off Keele Street, and he also made the audacious decision to take an engineering course at the downtown University of Toronto. By day he went to school, but he was also able to find a small job doing some cleaning in the evening. The Polish men in the house had told him about a Polish manager in a yacht club down by the lake. The man would pay cash for cleaners. Suleyman did the work, but the manager was evasive when it came to paying out the money. Suleyman had to pursue him to get paid. He got the money finally, and earning some cash "was a sweet thing." His landlady was also trying to take advantage of him, asking him to do cleaning jobs in other houses and then refusing to pay him. On October 20 he noted in his diary that he had "to be careful about these people who want to take advantage of others, who are cunning and dishonest. This monetary system makes people very selfish."

Suleyman, a committed socialist, would always cast a critical eye on the ravages of capitalism—how it relied on selfishness and strengthened that inclination, how it created systemic inequities and presented them as normal and natural. Suleyman had seen how the market system had been imposed on his own country, and he was always acutely aware of how it was being imposed in more subtle ways in Canada. It made him nervous.

Nonetheless, there were moments, evenings, when the freshness and freedom of the Canadian experiment made him feel better about his new home. He told his diary about one such evening in June—"the most beautiful night since I arrived"—when he attended a gathering in a downtown church to celebrate Refugee Rights Day. There were only two Kurds at the event, so Suleyman and a Kurd from Iran were asked to offer greetings on behalf of their community. Suleyman was clearly delighted by all the people from other Toronto communities who took part. Singer-songwriter Jane Field, a former high-school teacher who had been in a wheelchair since 1988—later a literacy worker at St. Christopher House—went on stage to sing some songs while accompanying herself with a guitar. Suleyman was impressed. A couple from El Salvador performed a dance, and later there was a singer from El Salvador. A folk group from Iran did traditional dances, and speaking in English they remarked on how Kurdish folklore was a symbol of struggle. A group from Viet Nam played music from their country, introducing all their members and the instruments they played. They also offered a greeting to the Kurdish people. "I will never forget how the Vietnamese people fought against the U.S.," Suleyman wrote that night.

On New Year's Eve 1991, almost nine months after his arrival at Pearson Airport, Suleyman sat alone in his room and reflected on both how slowly and how quickly time had passed. He was still arriving, still leaving, thinking about the future but not able to imagine it. It had been a long time since he had written in his diary. "Many good and bad things" had happened in that time, he wrote. It had been over a year since he had left his country and begun his travels through Europe to Ireland. Ten days earlier, on December 19, the first anniversary of his departure from Turkey, he had slept in and stayed at home to mark the occasion, although he was supposed to go to school to study English. He sat in his room intending to write an account of the many things that had happened in the past year, things that had shaped his life. He "was quiet and thoughtful" that day. But he found himself unable to write anything.

On that New Year's evening he did begin to write down some of his thoughts. He was the only person at home, and was watching coverage of the annual party at Nathan Phillips Square in the heart of the city. He thought about his journey from Ireland to Canada— "from a hostel in Ireland to Fern Avenue in Toronto." On the previous New Year's Eve in Ireland he had been invited to go to a pub. "This year no drinks, no girls, no party. I'm just sitting by myself in my room watching TV. Someone may think this is unusual, but everything seems okay with me. Is it? Everybody must be drinking and dancing and entertaining. Despite everything I am in fact happy." He was feeling good because he had been able to talk to his mother on the phone, and his friend Nurhan had called from Germany. "She would like to marry me. Everything is difficult for me . . . to make a decision about this proposal and my future."

The past year had been "a disastrous year for human beings," he thought. "The last socialist system collapsed. In 1991 the Kurdish people had many problems in Iraq because of the Gulf War. The fascists of that regime killed our people again. Many Iraqi Kurdish people crossed the Turkish border, and now they are living in camps in Turkey." Like many others on that evening, he had a resolution: "for a peaceful world without guns and war." But he also had a more immediate, personal hope: to pass the official Test of English as a Foreign Language and get his exams done for university—and maybe even get married. "I greet the New Year with my best wishes and love."

As it turned out, his goals for himself that year—not to mention his wishes for the world as a whole—would not be realized that quickly. His plans for school would be derailed by a social worker who said that it would be illegal for him to go to university full-time without a student permit and that until he became a landed immigrant he would have to pay foreign student fees.[4] Those fees, applied to foreign nationals and people without landed status, are significantly higher than the regular student fees. Suleyman could not possibly afford to pay them. His new social worker was not being particularly helpful. Once, when she visited him at home, she told him that the government was not giving him "money for sleeping all day." Now she was also telling him "something else"—that for the time being he could not fulfil his wish to go to university. Worse, she also told him that if he attended university illegally she would inform the Immigration office, and that could lead to deportation. Suleyman understandably felt threatened by the exchange.

One of his lowest moments would come in April 1992, when he got a poor mark on an essay he had handed in at the university. The professor was simply marking a paper. What the teacher did not see was the student who was extremely anxious, not just for a good mark but for a word of encouragement. At the time Suleyman thought he was doing pretty well because within a year of coming to Canada he was taking a course at a university and attempting to write a paper in English. However, the professor did not appreciate his written English and asked him to do the assignment all over again. That night, after eating his supper, Suleyman was beside himself with disappointment. "I was throwing the papers around my room and collecting them and then throwing them around the room again. I didn't know what I was doing and I lost my temper. I felt awful."

But he turned things around. In his own words, "I just tried to listen to myself." It was a Friday evening, and he decided to get out of his room and go play bingo. When he got back he wrote in his diary:

> I walked an hour on foot. I spent five dollars but won nothing. It was windy, stormy, rainy weather. I kept walking. It seemed like I was trying to punish myself in this weather. But now I seem kind of relieved. It seems the stressful moment is over. It seems I've beaten evil and depression. Now I can understand why people sometimes act like crazy and out of control. If you can't control yourself and don't have self-confidence you can easily go crazy.

He was alone, and he was struggling with himself. But for the first time he also began to articulate his troubles, getting a sense of how he was immersed in a system that makes people indifferent to each other. "The system makes people very selfish I think. People aren't interested in your problems. I have to struggle and fight against evil, calamity, and unfortunate things in the system—otherwise I won't be able to stay a healthy and normal individual."

At moments like this, and there would be many, Suleyman had an almost overwhelming sense of his own lack of power. He could not go ahead and he could not go back. Other people were making decisions about his future, and there seemed little he could do about it. Feeling vulnerable, he was searching for something, someone, to save him from getting lost in this uncertain future.

In January he had gone out one evening to a play called *Heaven's Gate and Hell's Flames* at an evangelical church on the Queensway, not far from his neighbourhood. He was intensely moved by the play, and especially by the spiritual feelings that he shared with the others in the audience. It was a moment of deep change for him.

> Absolutely I feel something strong about God. There's no dif-ference for me, whether in a mosque or church, whether people pray to him and cry, there's nothing wrong with that. I think our life is based on right and wrong things or sometimes we might be good or bad individuals. I think in Canada I did some-thing different from before. Tonight I prayed to God to change my life. I wanted to be born into his kingdom. I guess I deserve this.

One other moment in that time of living lonely stands out as a revelation of the kind of person Suleyman was, had been, and would be. On Sunday, July 1, 1992, he went to Queen's Park to cel-ebrate Canada Day with thousands of others. "There were big crowds. They were distributing fruit juice and other beverages," he wrote in his diary. While he was strolling around he noticed a small white dog trying to cross the busy street. Realizing that the dog was in danger, he hurried over and grabbed it, pulling it out of harm's way. At the same time he noticed a young woman and another man nearby who also saw what was happening. "But they didn't help," he noted. The woman came over and patted the dog. Apparently, because the dog was so friendly, the two people thought it was Suleyman's dog. He told the woman that the dog was not his—that he had only realized the dog was in danger and decided to intervene.

The girl asked Suleyman to entrust the dog to her, and he agreed. It turned out she was a hairdresser, working in a shop nearby, and they took the dog there. "I said I would sometimes come and visit the dog." But just then another woman came into the shop and asked about the dog. She turned out to be the dog's real owner, and was very upset. Suleyman apologized for the mix-up and left.

Gradually Suleyman had become friends with other Kurds, who would invite him for supper with their families. He started to attend some meetings of the Kurdish Association in Toronto, which included people not just from Turkey but also from Iran, Iraq, Syria, and Armenia. It was a small organization, hardly representative of the twenty million Kurds who identify with the homeland that had become spread over four countries. The Kurds are the largest ethnic group in the world without some national status.

One evening, after a meeting of the Kurdish Association, Suleyman went out for coffee with a few other Kurds from Turkey. A restaurant near the split between Roncesvalles and Dundas West had become their gathering place. It was owned by someone from their community. Once they were inside it could have been any coffee shop in Ankara or in the villages of eastern Turkey. The men began to discuss about how their interests were different from those of other Kurdish groups. Suleyman became aware of the number of Kurds arriving in the city, and he could see they were now in the same situation as he had been. "They are lonely and single and they suffer."

The casual conversation at the coffee shop became more focused and began to shape the idea of a Kurdish Turkish information centre. Suleyman and the others began to visit Kurdish families and ask them whether they thought there was a need for a centre aimed specifically at Kurds from Turkey. The response was overwhelming.

In August 1992 Suleyman and some of his friends established the Toronto Kurdish Community Centre. The group was able to pull together enough money to pay for the rental of a small storefront on Dupont Street. Out of almost nothing they created a space in which they could regain some dignity, some sense of community, as many of them prepared to have their refugee claims heard by representatives of the people of Canada. Now those who had closed the doors of their lives began to come out and meet other Kurds. Isolated and alone, they had felt like survivors of a political firestorm that no one in Canada had heard about, or cared to know about. As they began to gather, an ancient pride took hold—and divisions just as old.

For Suleyman the effort to start a centre for his people rekindled in him a passionate sense of mission. He remembered how abandoned and alone he had felt when he first arrived in the city, hungry and homeless, forced to pray in a mosque contrary to his beliefs. Almost daily, more Kurds were arriving in the city, fleeing from the brutality of the Turkish forces who were sweeping through the eastern provinces, trying to wipe out the possibility of any co-operation between the Kurdish villages and the Iraqi Kurds who were now there as a result of the first Gulf War.

Because his English was now more fluent than that of most of the Kurds in Toronto, it fell to Suleyman to find out how the Centre could become incorporated as a non-profit organization. He went down to the Ministry of Corporate Affairs to register the organization. The officers listed on the incorporation program were simply those who had met regularly at the coffee shop. It would prove to be a fateful decision. Suleyman Goven was listed as the president of the new Toronto Kurdish Community Centre.

Suleyman once again found himself daring to dream about his future. He would get his university transcripts from Turkey evaluated to see how many more courses he would need to take to become certified as an engineer. He would join a political party—his choice was the New Democratic Party—and eventually run for office. He would begin to get politicians and city councillors involved in the Centre. The Kurdish community would make its contribution to the political life of the city.

Suleyman had made his initial refugee claim shortly after his arrival in Toronto. His hearing was eventually scheduled for March 1993, some two years later. It was not an easy process, by any means. Some Kurds, less educated than Suleyman, did not know how to obtain the assistance of a lawyer; others were not able to distinguish between a good lawyer and the charlatans, the immigration consultants who swam like sharks around every refugee community. There was always the possibility of having a hearing before panel members who knew nothing about the complex realities of Turkey. Whatever the case, some Kurds from Turkey had been rejected by the Refugee Board and placed on a fast track to deportation back to Turkey. Everyone knew that any Kurd deported back to Turkey would never get out of the airport upon arrival in that country.

Suleyman had taken most of the initiative in making his refugee claim. He had filled out the application or Personal Information Form in which he gave his so-called "tombstone data," all of the important dates in his life history. He wrote down the list of events that had led him to leave his own country and the reasons why he needed the protection of Canada. His claim was to be heard by the Immigration and Refugee Board in order to determine if he was a refugee in the sense defined by the Geneva Convention. At the hearing he was assisted by a competent lawyer who helped him to articulate his claim to two thoughtful members of the Immigration and Refugee Board. He explained how his activities as a union leader had made him a target of the Turkish military, how an extreme leftist group had killed his father. In his case, fortunately, the panel members were aware of the risks faced by union leaders in Turkey and the price of opposing extremists. The documentation was in place. After being questioned for two hours Suleyman was told that he had been accepted as a Convention refugee. It was a clear and positive experience of justice within the Canadian system.

The decision gave Suleyman a sense that he could trust the judicial processes within Canada. He believed that this was a place where his human rights would be respected, that it was a place where he could fight for the human rights of others. He had been treated fairly and with respect and he resolved to become a good citizen, to treat others with fairness and respect.

• • •

Suleyman knew that things had not gone so well for other Kurds. Through the grapevine he had heard my name referred to as someone who might be able to help. "The Lady is helping the refugees." So Leddy became the Lady who could work miracles . . .

If only! If the Lady could do anything, it was only because she had joined others in the effort to found an organization called the Ontario Sanctuary Coalition.[5] The group had formed in 1992, when Christians who were working with refugees became increasingly alarmed by reports of genuine refugees who were being deported back to countries where they would face the serious possibility of being detained, tortured, or murdered. The members of the Coalition were a remarkable group of people, steady and faithful, who met on a weekly basis in the downtown Church of the Holy Trinity to address the crisis of deportations. Led by Michael Creal, an Anglican priest and former Dean of Humanities at York University, the group sifted through requests for help until its concern distilled around fourteen refugees (and their families) who were slated to be deported. Offering sanctuary to these people involved the simultaneous process of advocating on their behalf to political leaders and offering them a place within a church or religious building until their safety was ensured.

One of the "famous fourteen" was a young Kurdish man by the name of Sami Durgun. It was for his sake that Suleyman first came over to Romero House. As the years went by, the Coalition continued to act as a resource for refugees whose lives were threatened by deportation. From 1994 on, the safety of Suleyman Goven became a major (though not the only) concern for the Sanctuary Coalition. Even now the group continues to meet weekly and remains committed to ensuring that Suleyman finds the justice that he has been seeking in this country for such a long time.

ALL NIGHT

AT FIRST, for a while, Suleyman Goven was simply a blur of a face that came to the door of my office. At some point I noticed the eyebrows. It seemed that he always had someone else with him, someone who focused my attention more immediately.

"This is Sami. He was told he can return to Turkey because he won't have to speak Kurdish there. But anyone there will recognize his accent."

"This is Yilmaz. He has a nine-year-old son who is living with an old uncle in Turkey, and he needs to get him out."

"This is Twana. His wife is trapped in a village in the Kurdish area of Iraq."

On these occasions I began to take in the broad outlines of the landscape of the suffering of Kurds in Turkey, and then slowly the face that came to the door, and the person who came into my office, began to fill the frame of my mind. Soon he had a name, and soon I noticed he had a limp. Yet when he came we never talked about him, only the others.

Sometime in early 1994 I dropped into the Kurdish Community Centre, which had by then moved to a new location on Dundas Street West. It was a spare but proud little place, like every tiny toehold of identity that each immigrant group establishes when its people first arrive—though this one seemed particularly small compared to the others. The front room had a few old tables and straight-backed chairs. A small group of men sat there, drinking sweet tea. A room behind that had its floor covered with rugs and served as another gathering place. At the time I did not notice flags or pictures of Kurdish leaders. I recall the smile of Suleyman as he rose to greet me. He bowed and shook my hand. Before that I hadn't known he could smile. It was a wide and generous smile.

Occasionally, after that, I dropped over to the Centre with some clothes and food donated for refugees. The poverty of the Kurdish community was evident. The Kurds had no boots or gloves in the winter, and they wore heavy woollen pants even as the streets of Toronto started to steam. I never left the Centre without being offered a cup of spiced tea. One time Suleyman said to me, with a wink, "Sorry we don't have crumpets."

I asked him where he had learned his English. "It's very good," I said.

"I learned to speak English when I came here," he said, and our first real conversation began. He told me about his Turkish degree in mechanical engineering and how he had studied a bit of French at university.

"Did you work as an engineer?"

"Oh yes. I had a very good job with a mining research institute until I was put in jail."

I waited. It was his line to cross. And then he began telling me about how he had become active in the union movement, beginning in 1979. "I started to speak up," he said. "They picked me up and tortured me. They used electricity. That wasn't the worst thing. Even worse was when they beat my feet. The worst thing was hearing the screams of the other people in the corridors. Then they let me out. And I limped away."

After that he wanted to go back to work—he wanted to get married and have a family, he told me—but he was drafted into the Turkish army. He even became a lieutenant because of his education and because he did so well at the training school. "I was the best in my class," he said. "But they would never give me any position of real responsibility because of my arrests and because I was a Kurd. They used me. That's all. They sent me on assignments to areas that nobody else would go to because it was so cold. They even sent me to the Kurdish areas in the east. I could never have fought against my own people. Maybe they knew that.

"Anyway, it didn't last forever. I injured my elbow while playing on the soccer team of my army unit. That meant I could get a discharge from the army and go home and begin to look for a job. But eventually they came after me again when there were Kurdish uprisings in the east. They used electricity again and, worse, they beat my feet. It was then I knew I couldn't be safe in Turkey. It wouldn't matter what I did or didn't do. When I got out I used my rail pass to go through Europe and to get as far away as I could.

"I went to Ireland . . ."

"That's where my family came from."

"Oh, it's a great place," he said, with a smile. "The people were so friendly and the music was so happy. But—can you imagine?— they couldn't find one Kurdish translator in the whole of Ireland. This meant I couldn't have an interview for refugee status. So I came to Canada. It was my last hope."

I would hear this story several times, and each time it developed more layers.

"When did you come to Canada?"

"In 1991, and I've been accepted as a refugee, but I'm still waiting for my landed immigrant papers. They're pretty tough on the Kurds. I think they think we're all a bunch of terrorists just waiting to blow things up. I want to go to university so I can work here as an engineer. I've been accepted at the University of Toronto and McGill, but they say I have to be a landed immigrant first. So I spend my time here trying to help people in the community."

And that was what he was doing—listening to people who dropped into the Centre, helping to translate documents, organizing a demonstration against the Turkish Embassy in Ottawa. He was one of the most highly educated members of the Kurdish community, and the task of acting as the interlocutor with various agencies had fallen to him.

•   •   •

What Suleyman told me that day was only the first sketch of his story. It would be filled in and filled out in the following years and, sometimes, even falter. But at least now he was a real person to me, a person with a name and a face. I had seen him smile. He had dropped his guard.

One evening months later, on October 12, 1994, he came to the door of our kitchen in Romero House. I was cooking supper for our staff and was slightly startled to see the eyebrows come around the corner, after the office was closed. He didn't have anyone else with him.

This time he was not smiling. He seemed awkward, even ashamed, as he shifted from foot to foot.

"How are you?" he asked.

"Good," I replied.

"How are things at Romero House?"

"Good." I was a little startled. We had never talked about me that much.

"What are you doing?"

"Cooking supper."

"Good."

"So what's up, Suleyman?" I wanted to relieve us both of the burden of small talk.

"Are you busy tomorrow?" he asked. He sat down at the kitchen table and rubbed his hands on his knees.

"Yes, I am. Tomorrow's the day I teach at the university."

"You have to?" He seemed worried or puzzled. I could not tell which.

"Why? What's on tomorrow, Suleyman?"

"Well." He hesitated. "I got a letter from Immigration telling me that I should go in for my security interview. My lawyer just phoned to say she can't go, but that someone should go with me."

In the months I had known him he had never asked for anything for himself, and he would not do so now.

To this day I do not know why I responded so quickly, so easily. Maybe there are moments, like the blink of an eye, when everything you have become moves into a single point of focus. Someone turns to you and asks you for a kind of help you have never given before, and you know right away that much depends on your answer. It is a moment when your life moves in one way or the other.

This moment divides your life into everything that went before and all that follows after.

"I'll go with you," I said.

"But you have to teach. Your students. University is very important for them."

"And for you, too. I'll make arrangements for them if I'm late. How long will it take?"

"Well, they said to be there for nine in the morning . . . about two hours."

"No problem. I can easily make it for my 4:30 class." It all seemed so simple then. First I would go to the Immigration interview and then I would go off to the halls of learning: two very different worlds of meaning that still seemed connected by a sense of truth.[1]

• • •

Early the next morning I met Suleyman outside the Dundas West subway station. He was wearing a gleaming white shirt and his one good, very bright, red sweater. We went inside and he stood solidly in the middle of the westbound platform aisle.

"You know," he said, smiling slightly, "no one ever cancelled an appointment for me before."

In the subway car we were clumped together with people in suits on their way to work and teenagers in uniform, heading, I guessed, to the first class at Michael Power High School at the end of the subway line. Some of them had painted their fingernails black.

We got off at the Kipling station and walked through a parking lot and across the road to a tall white building with slats for windows. The only visible sign on the ground level was an arrow pointing to a coffee shop. On the door were small black letters indicating that this was the Canada Immigration Centre, Etobicoke.

Inside, in the waiting room, it was a typical Immigration Centre: the flag, the Canadian coat of arms, rows of seats, and two or three wickets with workers behind them. At that time of day—still well before nine—it was not too crowded, and we went directly to a wicket and presented Suleyman's call-in notice. The woman there took the notice, glanced at it, and asked us to have a seat.

While we waited I mentally ran through the outline of my class for later that day. I was treating all of this as a formality.

"Mr. Suleyman Goven. Please come to the wicket."

We walked in the direction of the wicket, but a young woman in a tailored suit intercepted us. "No. Come this way," she said. She led us off and then took out a plastic card and used it to open a door that had neither a handle nor a window. We were taken down a long corridor and then off to the right, to another door. This one opened with a handle. Inside was a large oval table, a boardroom type of table, with several chairs around it. A Canadian flag and the Canadian coat of arms dominated one of the walls.

A slight young man with straight blond hair and wire-rimmed glasses was already sitting at the table, with a couple of file folders in front of him. The young woman sat down beside him and instructed us to sit on the opposite side.

Each of them took out a small ID card case, opening them quickly, as if synchronized. Badges. "We work for the Canadian Security and Intelligence Service," one of them said. They gave their names, which didn't register in my mind.

"We're here today to conduct a security interview," the woman said. "Our recommendations will directly affect whether or not you receive landed immigrant status in this country. Is this clear?

You have someone with you. Is she a lawyer? Is she here with your permission, Mr. Goven?"

"Yes. She is a friend." I pulled out my business cards and gave one to each of them. I am sure that my name and position as director of Romero House meant nothing to them at the time.

"Are you sure you want her here?" asked the woman. "We will be asking some very personal questions, which may be embarrassing to you."

"I have nothing to hide."

The woman began to ask questions. She was polite, deferential. Opening one of the file folders, she slowly began to go through Suleyman's papers from his refugee claim, checking the details of his family history, birthday, the whereabouts of his relatives. Then she walked through the information form that Suleyman had filled out at the time of his refugee hearing. We could see that the form had been highlighted in pink in some places, yellow in others.

"You were in prison twice. What happened?"

"It wasn't that long. I got out alive."

"Why did they put you in prison?" she inquired politely.

"As far as I can tell, because I was a union leader."

"Were you a member of a terrorist group?"

"No." She checked a box on the page in front of her.

"Were you ever a member of the PKK?" She seemed to have done her homework. The PKK (Kurdistan Workers' Party) is a Kurdish resistance movement that had recently been involved in the bombings of some Turkish offices in Europe. The party had been banned in some European countries, but not in Canada.[2]

"No," answered Suleyman. "I have never been a member of the PKK."

"Are you sure?" She looked up at him, waiting.

I noticed that the slight, bone-edged man beside her was decidedly not looking at Suleyman. He was doodling on a piece of paper.

"Yes. I sympathize with the effort to get justice for the Kurds, but I do not support violent tactics."

"But you have been involved in demonstrations outside the Turkish Embassy in Ottawa," she noted as she opened another file.

"Yes," replied Suleyman. "I helped organize them. We wanted to protest what was happening to our families in Turkey. The villages burned. All the innocent people they have killed. They will not even let us speak our own language. We have a right and duty to protest."

"Of course you do." She smiled sweetly. She continued with her questions in this vein for some time. Finally, around eleven o'clock, she said, "I have no further questions." Glancing at her partner she asked, "Do you?"

Her colleague pulled a bundle of extra folders from the seat beside him. "A few."

After a short pause he said, "Now, Mr. Goven, you realize that if we find you credible and if you co-operate with us, we will recommend you for landed status?"

"Yes. I would like to be landed. I hope to get my engineering degree in Canada so I can work. I have been accepted to go to McGill, but I must be landed."

"We'll see about that."

The security officer took off his glasses and squinted. His mouth was tight and he talked with a discernible French accent. "You are an engineer, Mr. Goven. Now that would qualify you to build bombs, wouldn't it?"

"I never learned how to build bombs."

At that point I took out my notebook and began to make notes. It was an old habit I had developed during my time as a working journalist in the 1980s. I sensed something was coming down.

"But you were in the Turkish army. Didn't they teach you that? Didn't they teach you how to use weapons?"

"I learned how to use a gun, but they never gave me any sophisticated weapons because I was a Kurd."

"You went to Germany. What groups did you contact there?"

"A girl, an old friend from Turkey."

"Why did you go to Ireland? Did you make contact with the terrorists there? What did they teach you?"

Suleyman told them about his stay in Ireland, just as he had told me months before. I could see where this was all going in the mind of the agent. Here was a Kurd who had made several stops in Europe, possibly contacting different terrorist groups on his way to Canada.

"Did you make contact with the IRA? Did they teach you terrorist activities?" The officer's mouth got even tighter, his voice more monotonous.

"I only met a few people in Ireland. It was hard for me to speak. I couldn't find an interpreter. Listen—if I wanted to fight, I would have stayed in Kurdistan or I would have stayed in Europe. I just wanted some peace. I wanted some peace of mind."

"Do you belong to the PKK?"

"No."

The CSIS agent put his glasses back on. "But you said you sympathized with them. Doesn't that mean you are a member?"

"No. I sympathize with their goals but not their means." Suleyman placed his hands on the table. "How would you feel? How would you feel if your home had been destroyed? If your family had been killed? If your people were suffering?"

"You are here to answer questions, not to ask them." The bone-edged, precise man opened another folder and pulled out some photographs. He passed one of the photos over to Suleyman.

"Do you recognize this woman?"

"Yes, she's a journalist from Kurdistan who came to visit Canada with a delegation to explain the situation of our people to politicians here."

"This woman is a member of the PKK."

"She may be. But even if she is, what is the problem? The PKK is not a forbidden group in Canada. The government here recognizes that the PKK is trying to save the people from genocide. The world needs to hear about this."

"There was a demonstration at the Turkish Embassy in Ottawa and someone threw a stone. Did you know that?"

"I heard about it, but I wasn't there. I was doing a radio interview."

"Do you sympathize with such violence?"

"I don't support violent action. My father was killed by extremists."

Suleyman paused and looked down. This was news to me. He took his hands off the table. He clutched his hands tightly together until they turned almost white.

"Why were you made the leader of the Kurdish community here? Why would they trust someone who had been an officer in the Turkish army?"

"Well, I am one of the most educated persons in our community. As my English improved, I was able to help people. And I guess they like me. They are grateful."

"We have transcripts of phone conversations from your office."

"I have nothing to hide."

"Can you give us the names of PKK *members who are in the Kurdish community here? Remember that we will base our recommendation for landing on your replies."*

• • •

So there it was. You become an informant—spy on your community—and we will give you landed immigrant status.

So there it was. And there I was, writing down the sentence, the threat.

"I can't give you information I don't have," Suleyman replied. "But I would like to be landed. I have been waiting for years trying to do something with my life. I used to be able to build things. Now I am just picking up pieces."

Suleyman began to rub his knees with his hands. He crossed his arms.

The guardian of the files continued to question. At one o'clock we were allowed a ten-minute break to go to the washroom. There was no time for lunch. The questioning continued through the afternoon.

It had become an interrogation. At some point I was told that I could not intervene in any way during this "interview." Eventually my mind started to wander. My writing hand was feeling cramped. I noticed a picture of the Queen on a wall, and a plaque from Jean Augustine (the MP for the area) commending the Centre for its service to Canada. And where were we in this room, which had become a cell of the mind, a place where some human beings held absolute power over another human being who was virtually powerless?

I found myself pounding my fist down on the table. "Just a minute. Are you trying to say that the PKK is an illegal organization in this country? It is not. Even if Suleyman was a member, there is nothing illegal about that. You have no right to interrogate him in this way."

"Well, yes, you are quite right," the man said. His lips became a thin line. "You understand we have to protect the security of our country. We're just doing our job. We can't have people going around bombing innocent people."

"None of us want that. It's my country too," I said. I was seething by now. "Let me make it simple for you." I turned to Suleyman and asked, "Do you know of anything or anyone that would harm innocent people, children, in this country?"

"I don't have this information. If I did, I would do everything possible to prevent violence. I have seen too much violence. I have seen too many innocent . . ." Suleyman stopped.

The young woman intervened. "That will be it for today. We will send in our recommendation to Immigration."

The two agents picked up their files and walked out. It was now four in the afternoon. The interrogation had lasted almost seven hours, and it was too late for me to get to the students waiting for me at the university. The only thing I wanted to do was go home and write out my notes in detail. I had a sense that they would be important, somehow, somewhere.

I put my hand on Suleyman's shoulder. "I'm okay," he said as he got up and limped out. We went down the long corridor. An Immigration officer came and opened the door to let us out.

I suggested to Suleyman that we get a coffee at the little shop in the building. As we went outside the doors of the Immigration Centre and along the walkway to the coffee shop, Suleyman turned and pressed his forehead against the wall of the building. He pounded his fists once against the wall and then slumped down on his knees.

"I will never be safe," he muttered. Then, to my amazement, he gave out a long and low howl. It sounded like a dog lost out on the prairies or like a human being who has no words left for suffering. It would take years for me to truly understand that howl, and how it broke forth from long ago and far away.

AND HE STRUGGLED

O NE DAY when Suleyman Goven was eight years old he was tending sheep in the Dersim Munzur mountains of eastern Turkey. It was his father's flock, and he had been entrusted to their care. As the sheep were grazing up and down the mountainside near his village he saw two wolves circling the flock, drawing closer. He saw them bare their teeth, heard them growling, and was paralyzed with fear. This was the first time, he told me years later, that he experienced a sense of powerlessness flooding the reservoir of his soul.

Just then, the large family dog appeared and chased the wolves away.

There would be other times when the dog did not arrive and the sheep were destroyed by the wolves, and times when guard dogs were killed in the struggle against predators. Whenever any of the sheep were killed, Suleyman would weep. For him, they were part of the family.

The sheep and other animals became characters in the allegorical tales that his great-grandmother told the children in the Goven family. "I still remember the whole family gathered around the stove," Suleyman told me. "My great-grandmother would tell us stories about the animals. I really loved the stories. I would laugh and sleep nicely."

• • •

The district traditionally known as Dersim spreads out over an almost inaccessible area of high, snow-capped mountains and deep ravines.[1] Ragged trees cling to the sides of steep slopes. The remoteness of the village of Zarik, where Suleyman grew up, fostered a fierce sense of independence and protected it from some of the violent political upheavals that had erupted throughout the region— some, but not all. Travellers to the region have described it as poor and barren. The officials and politicians of the Turkish government have described it as backward and even uncivilized. Indeed, most of the people in the rest of Turkey thought of it as a God-forsaken area run by feudal warlords.

The landscape of Suleyman's childhood added a certain gravity to his imagination. As a child he ran along the backbone of the mountains in the traditional leather shoes and baggy pants of Kurdish peasants. One day he would be high on the mountains, looking down on the buildings in his village and the tiny specks of life in motion. Another day he would be down below at the foot of the hills, feeling humbled, surrounded and enveloped by something vaster, more solid than himself.

It is still the place that Suleyman calls home. He thrilled at the blue lakes and the big waterfall that came down from the mountains, the running water and "the extraordinary beauty of Mother

Nature." He watched the deer on the mountains and saw "flowers of every colour, bees, and running water." He collected eggs from the pheasants, ate various flowers, listened to the birds chirping. He picked mushrooms by the springs and the waterfalls. The rivers were full of trout. Besides sheep his family had a dog, cat, horse, chickens, goats, and cows. He and the other children in his family "were raised to be friends with the animals and with nature."

The winters could be tough. "There was brilliant snow," he said, "sometimes two and a half metres in the winter, which could cover over the houses in the village. The people had to break the ice in the streams for drinking water." Suleyman remembered his father taking the goats to the forest in the wintertime and keeping busy cutting trees for fuel. "We would carry our wood on horseback and pile it up close to our house. It was fun to place the logs in the stove and eat bread and cheese and onion." He recalled how they used to have to get up on the roof of the house in the winter and "throw" the snow off. They had to make a path through the snow so the livestock could get to their drinking water. If there was a heavy storm the family became isolated from the other villagers nearby.

Suleyman grew up as the oldest of ten children—there were two others who died when they were young. The marriage of his parents had been arranged between the two families when his mother was only fourteen, and it was several years after the marriage before his mother had her first child. Suleyman described his mother as "peaceful, honest, and very brave." Later on, when he was imprisoned, she would walk six hours to bring him some fruit and even went to visit the commander and prosecutor to ask for her son's release. The Canadian security agents who would later hold Suleyman's freedom to travel in their hands had no sense that one of his deepest hopes was to get his landed papers because then he would be free to go home to see his mother before she died.

His father was a complex figure in his life. "He was very brave when he was young," Suleyman explained to me. "He stood up for injustice when others tried to take our highlands, but then he was threatened by leftist extremists." Later his father became timid and frightened, nervous and easily upset. When Suleyman was a young man and became politically involved, his father disowned him and would not speak to him for two years. Through the years Suleyman worried about him. He knew that his father had suffered a lot in his life. His father sometimes isolated himself for long periods of time, going off to the barn and other haunts. He took his fears out on his wife, beating her. Suleyman witnessed a lot of arguments between his parents, and later attributed at least some of the conflict and tension to the bitterly hard work of the lives they led. "I think their fighting stemmed from exhaustion. I still wonder how my mother managed to look after all those children."

The large family was pressed together in a two-storey brick house. The barn, with the animals in it, was on the ground floor. The second floor had one room for the whole family to sleep in and another room for guests. All of the family shared in the work, according to age and ability.

In the summertime the big job was cutting hay and laying it out in the sun to dry. "I sometimes dream of my father and of a whole field of grass that still has to be cut," Suleyman told me. Villagers would compete with each other in cutting and hauling hay from the commons. "We would go to the mountains in the morning and return late afternoon. A good meal was ready for us." The births of sheep, goats, and calves were moments of amazement and delight for the children. The whole family helped to look after the young animals. "The children could drink the fresh milk and I could play with them." Everyone was filled with sadness when, as sometimes happened, the newborn did not survive.

His family also had honey bees, and Suleyman later related how one of his favourite pastimes was to watch the bees when they were "carrying a variety of colourful pollen on their wings. We knew the honey was natural, made by the master craftsmen. I was surprised that the bees never stung my father even though he did not cover his face. I think the bees recognized their owner. They sometimes tried to sting me but I managed to run away."

In those early days he was learning other things too, about girls. As he told me: "The girls and boys started playing at an early age under the trees, on the grass, along a stream or lake or in a forest. We would feel first, touching. I do remember that I and my uncle's daughter would pretend that we were husband and wife even though we did not know the meaning of marriage. It was a childish thing. The hay was an excellent place for lovers but I did not have sex until I came out of prison and started working for the railways in 1984."

For Suleyman, Dersim was where he learned about the sense of lurking danger that was all around. "Walking through the mountains at night was a scary experience. I felt that the giant shadows were walking with us. The wolves were howling."

A rough kind of justice prevailed in the mountains of Dersim. On one occasion Suleyman was tending to the flock of goats with his uncle's daughter. They got into a fight, and the girl accused him of killing a goat. Her father decided something needed to be done about this, and at nine years of age Suleyman found himself facing a judge, accused by his own uncle. It would be the first of many false accusations, and this one affected Suleyman deeply. Fortunately, the judge dismissed the charges and told the uncle that he should be ashamed of bringing his nephew to court on a false pretext.

When Suleyman misbehaved—like the time when he and his cousin stole cucumbers and tomatoes from a neighbour's garden, or when the boys refused to herd the animals—his father would grab him around the neck, as if to choke him, or beat him. His mother would usually intervene to prevent the worst.

One day, exploring in the mountains, he came across a gypsy camp. The gypsies saw him and surrounded him, accusing him of planning to steal things from their camp. They began discussing his punishment. One of them, a big guy, started hitting his head with a big ring—with Suleyman "crying and swearing" that he was just wandering around. After a while the big guy loosened his grip and Suleyman was able to run away. "I nearly lost my life that day."

• • •

When he was young Suleyman constantly heard of the many chapters in the long story of the suffering of Kurds and Armenians in the area. The name of their village, Zarik, came from the Armenians who had once settled and lived in the area. The village had the ruins of two Armenian churches, and more Armenian graveyards than Kurdish. In Persian mythology, Zarik (or Zarich) is an evil spirit that serves his creator, Ahriman.

The massacre of the Armenians lies deep in the memory of the people of eastern Turkey. By the early twentieth century, the major part of Armenia's historic lands—with a population of more than four million—belonged to Turkey. The Turks, under pressure in the First World War, were unsure of the allegiance of the predominantly Christian Armenians, and in 1915 Turkish nationalists killed somewhere between 600,000 and 1.5 million Armenians.[2] At the time the U.S. ambassador to Turkey, Hans Morgenthau, tried to bring the mass murder of the Armenians to the attention of the world, but to no avail. The world took so little notice that the incident served Hitler with a great precedent, an instructive lesson of the world's possible reaction if it heard about his genocidal plans for the Jews. Speaking to his police officers, Hitler asked the rhetorical question, "Who today remembers the Armenians?"

In some places the Kurds actively participated in the genocide initiated by the Turkish armed forces, but the villagers of the Dersim area, perhaps because of the large number of intermarriages, perhaps because of their reluctance to co-operate with the Turks, helped many Armenians escape over the mountains to Russia. A U.S. missionary working in the area noticed the courageous efforts of the Kurds of Dersim: "When it came to dealing with a defenseless Armenian fugitive, the instinct of the noble savage is to save rather than wantonly to destroy this neighbor against whom he has no grudge."[3] The Kurds, apparently, were noble savages.

Some ninety years later, in Canada, the ghosts of the Kurds and Armenians of Dersim would haunt the House of Commons in Canada as it debated the memory of the Armenian genocide.

The next time the Turks came to the Dersim area with mass murder in mind was in 1937. By the 1930s, as Dutch anthropologist Martin van Bruinessen points out, Dersim was "the last part of Turkey that had not been effectively brought under central government control." This was at least in part because of its forbidding terrain and the culturally distinct population living on that land—peoples, according to van Bruinessen, divided into a large number of "small tribes." Among these various groups, he points out, there were "perpetual conflicts . . . often taking the form of protracted feuds," and "the only law they recognized was traditional tribal law."[4] This state of affairs was anathema to the project of the new Turkish nationalism of Kemal Atatürk—a project demanding that any serious cultural or religious differences in the country be subsumed in the new secular state that was being built up out of the ruins of the Ottoman Empire. As one step in this project the Turkish government, attempting to gain control over the area, gave the district of Dersim the new name of Tunceli in 1935 (though many people still use the old name). Suleyman summarized the political realities with this metaphor. "They wanted to have a rose without thorns."

The Dersim area was the traditional homeland of the Alevi Kurds, who were different both culturally and religiously. They had always been considered unruly, following ancient forms of tribal justice rather than more modern forms of organized justice. Suleyman's family was part of the Alevi religious clergy, and his family tree was written on a piece of deer leather with golden letters. As he grew up and learned more about his family, Suleyman realized that all the tribal groups in Zarik were related to each other and went back to Kurds who had migrated to the district from Iran.

The Alevi religion contains elements of Sufism and even Christianity. The language of their liturgy is Turkish as opposed to the majority Sunni or Shia use of Arabic. The Alevis do not emphasize the times of prayer during the day or other types of regular rituals; instead they stress a more intuitive faith, one oriented towards the importance of community. They consider the pilgrimage to Mecca an external pretence; the real pilgrimage is internal, in one's heart.[5] The only thing that bothered Suleyman about the Alevi religion was the practice of sacrificing animals. His people were forbidden to hunt animals, but they would sacrifice them when a relative died and then give the meat to the poor. "According to our faith our villagers never hunted deer or rabbits or pheasants," Suleyman told me. "My father used to go hunting but then he had a dream of the deer they killed and he swore not to hunt any more. But my father used to sacrifice animals in the month of Muharram and Hizir. He asked me to stand and watch when he sacrificed an animal but I found it very gruesome because I considered them part of my family."

It would be the Alevi Kurds who were sacrificed to some strange secular idol in the massacre of Dersim. Because of the remoteness of the area, the Turkish forces were able to do what they wanted in 1937 beyond the scrutiny of the world. In any case, Europe itself was seized at the time with the prospect of war.

In 1937–38 the Turkish government carried out an unrelenting campaign of pacification against a rebellious population of Alevi Kurds in Dersim. The Kemalist regime wanted to subdue what it saw as an anarchic, uncooperative part of its national territory by imposing law and order and taxes. In the process, according to writer Mehrdad R. Izady, the army used "every weapon in its arsenal, including poison gas, heavy artillery, and even primitive bomber aircraft." Some men in the area gave battle, while women and children took refuge in deep caves. In some cases, according to reports, the army bricked up the entrances to the caves; sometimes they lit fires outside caves to suffocate the people inside. Izady describes other results of the campaign:

> Accounts abound of refugees immolated in woods, collective suicides of Kurdish villagers throwing themselves off cliffs, and

women and girls drowning themselves in rivers from fear of rape. Darsim was so thoroughly and ruthlessly devastated that the Turkish press notes, "*Delenda est Darsim*, or, "Darsim is no more," echoing the words of the Roman general Scipio two thousand years earlier on his destruction of Carthage.[6]

Suleyman grew up hearing both the tragic and "heroic" stories of those bitter days. He listened to the story of Seyit Riza, a leader in the area who had shared the same family tree. Seyit Riza had been among the first to be hanged in 1937. The family was never able to recover the body. "I heard of one of my relatives who stopped a whole unit at a mountain pass," he told me. His parents, children at the time, went off to hide in the caves with the older women. Later his parents would tell him about how they ate soil and roots to survive, and about how four hundred men, women, and children— many of them connected to his family—were massacred in a cave. As the story goes, "The blood mixed with the stream of the Munzur River." One child survived because he was covered by a dead body.

"I was told that the young Kurdish girls were raped by the Turkish soldiers viciously and that many girls jumped off the cliffs so they wouldn't be caught by the Turks," Suleyman said. "They massacred Kurds regardless of their age or gender because they were considered infidels and the enemy of the state and wild bandits." His grandfather and other relatives were arrested on suspicion of killing Turkish army officers. Luckily for them, while they were awaiting execution, Suleyman noted, "those who killed the Turkish military officials were caught and the execution did not take place. Otherwise, I would not be writing these lines."

The figures for the massacre vary from an official number of 12,000 to the local people's estimate of 70,000. Thousands more were either banished or fled the area to find safety. "Some of our people died of diseases along the way," Suleyman said. "I was told that two young girls from my family got lost and never were found. My family was sent to Bursa, and after the ban was lifted they returned to Dersim in the east."

• • •

Where do you bury 70,000 people? The earth itself is choked with the memory of suffering. The dead reach up and become leaves of grass, sheaves of wheat, chickens that feed, and a young boy running along the mountain paths.

Going to school meant learning about some of the realities of being a Kurd in Turkey. Many of the Kurdish children from the villages were encouraged or even forced to attend the primary, middle, and high schools. These were residential schools where the Kurds were to be assimilated into the Turkish state—the entire education system was geared towards making Kurdish children into good Turks. To achieve this end, the Turkish government employed Kurdish teachers who worked at eradicating the Kurdish accent and educating students in the ways of being Turkish. Suleyman started primary school at age five, and the harsh environment at the school he attended—a boarding school in Ovacik, about five to six hours' walk from Zarik—resembled that of a military training camp as much as a school. If the kids were caught speaking their own language, the teacher would place their hands on a hot stove— something that happened to Suleyman, several times. He remembered teachers pressing his eyeballs and beating him on the back. One day at the primary school the treatment was so bad that he escaped from the school and ran home, where he hid in the hay in the family barn. He stayed there for so long that he began to wonder if he would starve. His mother came and found him and urged him to go back to school.

When Suleyman returned home during the school holidays, his family teased him about having an accent and said he was forgetting his own language. The longer he was away at school, the more he lost his ability to speak Kurdish. His family would tease him that he was reading all these books but not able to speak his own language. They also teased him about all the girls who were eyeing him.

Nevertheless, Suleyman excelled in school. Wherever he went he became the top of his class. Was this ambition or just plain talent? During his early years at school, he simply bent to please the teachers and was obedient. That attitude underwent a change when he went off to middle and high school. The boarding school was located in a remote area some thirty kilometres from the provincial centre of Malatya, a relatively large city famous for its fresh and dried apricots. It was another cruel educational environment, but he delighted in becoming the best runner, a fast runner. He won a number of medals and was the number one runner in the region. He placed fourth in a 4,000-metre cross-country competition held in the capital city of Ankara. A team from his school once captured second place in the national championship. Maybe they were helped by the coaches' strategy of making them run through the snow to build up their endurance.

Suleyman told me about being in middle school and hearing the news that three leftist leaders—Deniz Gezmifl, Yusuf Aslan, and Hüseyin Inan—had been hanged in the capital city. No one in his group knew why they had been executed, but they did know that these men were respected people. "The older students told us they were brave and courageous and they were fighting for us." It was a defining moment for young Suleyman.

When he was still relatively young his family began to pressure him to get married. One of his uncles, whom he loved greatly, was killed in a car accident and the family began to talk about Suleyman marrying the widow, which would not have been unusual at the time. It was considered a responsibility to marry the widow of your brother or even your uncle—and to look after her.

It was at this point that Suleyman began to rebel. He realized that he could end up marrying his aunt or a girl he did not like. During his second year in high school, with a possible marriage in mind his mother asked him to go to see her uncle's daughter, who was living in a nearby town. He went on foot, walking for ten hours to the village. His great-grandmother—the one who had told him wonderful tales about the animals when he was young—asked him to elope with the girl because a lot of young men wanted her. "But I told her that I was a student and had plans to study at the university. The girl did not want to wait."

The high school itself began to reflect a swirl of events that were catching the country up in a political vortex. In the 1970s Turkey was torn by a series of strikes and demonstrations. Inflation soared, and the poor got poorer. Student groups and unions demonstrated regularly, and the government became more and more ineffectual. The school administration reflected the increasingly fascist tendencies in the country and tried to rein in the students who dissented. Most of the students belonged to the right-wing Nationalist Movement Party (MHP), and they were on the lookout for troublemakers. The MHP was so openly fascist that it declared that democracy was the invention of the Jews.

For the first time, Suleyman started reading leftist literature. He became involved in a demonstration organized by some of the older students. The students marched through the night all the way from the school to the city of Malatya, where the police were called in to stop the protesters. Suleyman was among those arrested and carted off to the police station. There the police officers did more than question him—they summarily punished him, striking his palms and different parts of his body with truncheons, causing swelling. On the following day they delivered him to the school, and the administrators decided to suspend him for two months. It would be the first of many interruptions in his education.

When he returned to classes he found the students in the MHP terrorizing the leftist and Kurdish students. At night in the dorms, after the lights went out, they would attack. The coach of the cross-country team tried to protect his valued runner from the abuse, which only led to more problems: word went around the school that Suleyman was co-operating with right-wing students.

By the time he finished high school, Suleyman had begun to identify himself as a leftist. The situation in Turkey had become so polarized that it was impossible not to get drawn into politics.

• • •

At age sixteen, when he finished high school, Suleyman was one of only three students from his area who were accepted into university. But for that he needed money, and his father was reluctant to help—or even to see him leave home once again. He might have been worried about the student unrest that was taking place throughout the country. Or he might simply have wanted to keep another hand around home to help with the farming. In any case,

his father went into a rage. "He punched and slapped me," Suleyman said. "He started chasing me through the hills in his bare feet."
Suleyman made his way to the high plateau where some of the villagers had set up their tents, and his father found him there. A relation, a woman, stepped out and stood between Suleyman and his
father, preventing further harm. Finally, after a change of heart,
Suleyman's father gave his son his blessing and some money to register at university.

Suleyman left for Adana, a large port city to the south, and
enrolled in a four-year engineering course. But again his way was
blocked. The MHP students had the authority to confirm registra-
tions and were stopping anyone who did not agree with them,
which included Suleyman.

The students who had been excluded began to meet and organize. Early one morning seventy-five of them entered the university together, against considerable opposition, and took refuge in
one of the buildings. The MHP students started throwing rocks and
stones at them and broke the windows of the building. The police
arrived and arrested everyone. Some of the members of Suleyman's
group had been badly injured. All of the students, from both sides,
eventually ended up in court, with each side blaming the other.
The judge did not believe the MHP story; he could plainly see the
evidence of the wounds of the students who had tried to go to the
university.

The incident and its result encouraged the students who did
not agree with the fascist tendencies of the MHP. Throughout the
country, there were mass demonstrations against the staggering
levels of unemployment and the austerity programs that the country was taking up, pressured by the International Monetary Fund
(IMF). The leftist movement on campus began to gather strength

and grew daily. The students met early every day and went together to the university, often singing songs of social protest.

Along the way Suleyman became one of the leaders in the student movement. He was recognized, targeted. One day in 1979 he and his friends were attacked by MHP activists. "I saw one of the MHP thugs sticking a knife into the stomach of one of my best friends," Suleyman said. He defended his friend with his fists, saving him from further damage, and turned to fight off another attacker, the head of the fascist group. Somehow he and his friends were able to get away, but when they were scrambling out of the building Suleyman realized that his body was soaked in blood. He and the others made it to the hospital. Today, he said, "I still have four scars as a result of this attack." His group took an official complaint to the police about the attack, but none of their adversaries were charged, and they were still able to attend classes.

Attending university involved more than fighting fascists, going to classes, and writing exams. Every day Suleyman got up early and worked in a restaurant to put himself through school. He was not only the helper and bottle washer at the restaurant but also the waiter and janitor. He and some friends rented a house together. There were the usual dalliances with young women. It seems someone was always trying to set him up with a girl, and he was glad to be set up. One friend took him to his house and introduced him to "a very beautiful girl" and asked him if he wanted to marry her. Later Suleyman did not know why he didn't say yes—but he did know that he was so preoccupied with this dazzling girl that he almost got hit by a car after he left the house. During his university years he had a close friend who had been at his high school. This friend's sister, yet another beauty, fell in love with him, but Suleyman did not think he should get involved with the sister of one of his best friends. (Later he realized "this was nonsense.") "She locked herself in a room and started crying and calling me heartless. I still feel guilty about not responding to her true love."

It was not an easy time to think ahead, to what came after university. It seemed possible that the government would fall, and the world would be turned upside down. The period between the 1960s and 1980s in Turkey was marked by periods of political instability, with military coups occurring in 1960 and 1971—and one to come in 1980.

• • •

In the summer of 1979 Suleyman began working full-time as a railway repairman for MTA (Mineral Research and Exploration Institute) while continuing to finish his studies. After six months on that job he was elected as a local union leader for the three provinces of Adana, Mersin, and Hatay. It was a position he took very seriously.

He had read in the literature being circulated around leftist and union circles how leaders had to earn the respect and trust of the workers. He resolved to do just that, and within six months they had "blessed" him. His new role as a leader gave him an identity, a feeling of responsibility for the workers. He had been summoned. The election to the position of union leader had, in fact, given him a sense of vocation and it would lead him along a road less travelled, a road more dangerous, destination unknown.

The year of his election would prove to be a momentous time in Turkey. By 1979 the country had reached a crisis point. It had also become increasingly important to U.S. foreign policy interests in the region, especially with the collapse of the Shah's regime in Iran and the Soviet invasion of Afghanistan. In March 1980 the U.S. government signed a new "defence and economic co-operation treaty" with Turkey. From that point on U.S. armed forces were able to use and build military bases in the country. In return the Turkish government received weapons systems worth $9 billion from the United States and got a further $6.5 billion in financial support to purchase U.S. military equipment.

On the morning of September 12, 1980, Suleyman was watching TV and saw the announcement of a military coup. He listened to the speeches of the generals and the sounds of nationalist songs. Almost immediately army tanks rolled into working-class neighbourhoods. Prominent intellectuals and dissidents were arrested. In the first six months after the coup, an estimated 123,000 political prisoners were jailed. There were numerous assassinations and military executions. In the jails, military installations, and police stations, torture was used, not so much to extract information as to destroy the morale of any opponents of the new military regime.[7] At least fifty people were tortured to death.

In the eastern Kurdish provinces, which had already been under martial law for two years, the military went on a rampage of rape, torture, and executions. In regions such as Dersim, the military banned the use of the Kurdish language and Kurdish names. It was probably only a question of time until Suleyman Goven would see the wolves circling his flock once again.

On a foggy morning of February 1981, six months after the coup, Suleyman arrived at work together with the other employees on his shift. He was the leader of a union called Dev-Maden-Sen, the mining workers union. The police were waiting with a list of the names of twenty-five workers. Later on, looking back, Suleyman said he suspected that the list had been provided by the Institute's administration. The twenty-five workers were all taken to a big room in the police headquarters and then hived off and interrogated separately in adjacent rooms. Some of those arrested were union activists, but most were simply ordinary union members.

Sitting with the others, awaiting his turn to be questioned, Suleyman stood up and made it known that he would never submit. "I wanted to show the workers that I deserved to be their leader and that I would not bow to our oppressors." He had a strong sense of what was likely to happen. He understood that most of the others would weaken and betray each other and him under duress. True enough, one of his comrades, a young woman, told the police that Suleyman was the head of Halkin Kurtuluşu (People's Liberation), a group that the government considered to be very dangerous. Suleyman could hear her voice as she talked. Then they took her away.

"They picked out the weak ones, who betrayed us easily." In the end the workers admitted whatever the masters of torture wanted them to say. They all confessed that Suleyman was the leader of the People's Liberation. Then the police officials came for Suleyman. As he later described it, "They hit my head against the wall several times, punched and squeezed my testicles. They said they would castrate me. I refused to co-operate. Then they used electricity."

His forehead was in a terrible state when they delivered him back to his cell. He had a terrible headache, but was otherwise alright. Later his captors took him up to another floor that was home to the security department. "They wanted to trap me when I was weak physically, but I was never weak psychologically. They tried to play good cop bad cop with me. The most painful torture was then, when they hit the swollen soles of my feet. I felt my heart was breaking into pieces."

During the torture session Suleyman was blindfolded. But at one point the blindfold slipped and he could see his tormenters. They had pretended that they were military officials, but he became certain that they were actually members of the security forces. "They were the secret police. One of them was called Umit, and had a puffy face—he was a blond man—the other was called Haydar."

The beating of feet, or falaka punishment, is one of the most effective means of torture. The nerves in the feet are extremely sensitive, the blood vessels build up pressure under the toenails, and often the toenails burst away. The damage to the feet can last a lifetime, and today Suleyman still has two black toenails. Years later he told me: "I was eighteen years old. I felt absolutely powerless, a slave in their hands. But I felt I owed the workers something and that I had to be loyal to them even if they were not loyal to me. I would not betray them even if they betrayed me. I would lead them, even in jail."

In Turkey he was able to see the faces and learn the names of his tormenters. It would not be so in Canada.

After forty-five more days in the detention centre and more torture, Suleyman and the others went before a military prosecutor. The decision had already been made: Suleyman was to be moved to a military jail. "I was shocked, as I had never admitted anything. It was clear there were new rules or no rules. The punishment did not have to fit the crime. It was a situation in which the guilty felt no remorse and the innocent were made to feel guilty." He asked why he was being sent to jail, because he had not admitted to anything. The prosecutor simply said that the police wanted him sent to jail.

Suleyman would be in a military prison in Adana for the next four and a half months. He began writing poetry at that time, but all the poems had to be destroyed before the regular searches of his cell. The poems were dangerous memories of his village, his place in the world. This would become a pattern in his life. Whenever he felt under enormous stress or weighed down with loneliness, he would write. When he was happy or things were going well, he would not—unless the happiness held a revelation.

After their time in detention most of the people who had denounced Suleyman recanted and said they simply did it because of the torture. He forgave them. He understood that it had less to do with their weakness and more to do with the power of pain to destroy not only the body but the soul as well. Had it destroyed something or someone in Suleyman as well?

• • •

During the past few years I have had the opportunity to live with, talk with, a number of people who have been tortured. Torture is not an abstract issue for me. Torture has a name and a face, and sometimes he or she lives in the same house as I do. I have heard him scream in the night; I have seen her frozen in mute fear. We can dwell side by side, but we live in different worlds—in different but not separate worlds.

I have yet to hear any reputable psychologists say that they really understand torture and its effects on both the perpetrators and the victims. Still, a few things can be said about it. For example, torture is sometimes used to extract information but it is more often used to destroy the inner core of a person or the identity and purpose of a community or group. Torture is used to demoralize human beings.

I have learned that under torture almost everyone cracks. Almost everyone betrays whomever or whatever they hold dear. This does not mean that the person is weak; it does indicate the immense and destructive power of torture. One refugee described the experience of torture as a process of being turned into Jell-O inside. He was afraid of unbuttoning his coat for fear that his insides would fall out.

The effects of torture vary depending on the type of person, their previous experiences, and, most importantly, their understanding of why they were tortured. It seems that the effects of torture are most devastating on those who have no understanding of why they were tortured. They were simply in the way, in the wrong place and the wrong time. This makes it much more difficult to understand what is happening or to place it within any framework of meaning.

Suleyman was terribly tortured during the time at police headquarters and later at the military prison. He was wounded and left limping. However, he understood why he was suffering. He was a Kurd, born to resist and to struggle. He had socialist convictions and he believed he was called to lead—even unto death. When such suffering is encompassed by a sense of meaning and purpose, there is always the possibility of redemption.[8] A person who has been tortured will never be the same, and it is an immense relief for them when they settle with this reality. The core of human trust and tenderness is broken severely, perhaps completely. Still, although the past cannot be changed, the future lies ahead; and it can infuse the past with a sense of meaning and purpose.

• • •

The only visitor Suleyman was allowed during his dark months in the detention centre was the young human rights lawyer Elif Tuncer. He told her that he did not need a lawyer because he had done nothing wrong. She told him that his friends had asked her to represent him. She was brave, feisty, human.

After Suleyman was released a friend by the name of Ali Adak looked after him and tried to nurse him back to health. Later on Suleyman recalled: "I was exhausted. I was in really bad shape. On the other hand I was proud of myself. I had survived. I had thought I would be killed. There were other friends who were killed. The memory of that time never goes away." It is there, he said, like the damage in his toenails. From that time, he became a man with a limp.

Nevertheless, he did pick himself up and try to walk again. He was free, but he had lost his job with the Mineral Research and Exploration Institute; and he had lost friends. The purge in Turkey had frightened many people, and some of his former friends were afraid to talk with him.

He had, not surprisingly, lost his sense of security. Friends at the MTA told him that the police continued to visit the workplace and to ask about his whereabouts. "I became a fugitive," he said. "Ali was my big brother." Ali encouraged Suleyman to finish his studies in the engineering department because he still had two courses to get through. But when he went to the university Suleyman noticed that he was being followed by undercover police. Worse, when he finally went to write an exam, they stopped him and arrested him.

Once again he ended up in the security department, where he was detained and tortured for ten days. This time he was released without charges. He was finally able to write and pass his exams in 1982 and become qualified as an engineer.

He decided to return to Zarik, although he was not sure he would be welcomed. His father—perhaps leery of Suleyman's political involvement and afraid of what it would mean for the family—had told him not to come home.

On the day that Suleyman re-entered the family home, no one was there. When he went to wash his face and hands in the stream by the house he noticed that the guard dog was standing very close to him. He held his breath. The dog generally attacked anyone from outside the family, and Suleyman was afraid that he had become a stranger, an enemy, and feared that the dog would attack him. Instead the dog jumped up and began to lick his face. The dog recognized Suleyman as friendly, as local.

The time at home was the beginning of a kind of healing. He went back out into the fields to work at cutting the grass and wheat. He went back to watching the bees. "My mother and I would visit the tomb of one of our saints," he remembered. "We would pray there overnight. People who visited the tomb were looking for a cure for their problems." All the time he continued writing poems, scribbling them out in a notebook. Later, after he had to leave once again, his mother was afraid that the military would raid the house and she destroyed the book of poems.

Then, in a rather bizarre turn of events, Suleyman Goven, enemy of the state, was drafted into the Turkish army. He reported to the recruitment office in Ovacik, where the authorities saw that there was still an arrest warrant out for him. As a result he found himself sent off to a civilian prison, where he would remain for another two months. His mother would walk five to six hours to bring him food, dairy products, and fruit. She complained to the public prosecutor and demanded that her son be released. He was let go, and he was now "free" to do his basic training to become an officer in the army.

During a ten-day leave before joining his unit, Suleyman contacted a matchmaker, who was also one of his best friends, who took him to meet a Kurdish Alevi girl living in Erzincan, about seventy kilometres north of Zarik. They liked each other and quickly arranged an engagement ceremony. On the very day of that special event—with the ceremony in progress—he had to leave his fiancée behind and rush to the bus terminal to depart for Van (a Kurdish province), where he would have to complete his military service.

The government policy was to draft all Kurds in order to make them into "good Turks." Once again Suleyman moved to the top of his class and was made a lieutenant in the Turkish army—though the Turks never really gave Kurds any real responsibility, and that was true in the case of Suleyman as well. "We were stationed in the east," he said, "but nothing much happened." When he got injured in an army soccer game he was discharged, after only a year and two months of service.

That stint in the Turkish army left him with some peculiar memories. He became aware of not just "homosexual activity but other kinds of relationships as well"—in particular, relationships with animals. "For instance, the Commander of the fourth unit had a female dog. It would not be an exaggeration to say that almost every soldier had relations with his dog." He also noticed how "the soldiers in the unit criticized the officers who swore at their wives and mothers and beat them mercilessly."

After being discharged from the army in 1984, Suleyman went about the business of trying to get a job. The greatest impediment was the record of his arrests. However, his mother contacted a distant relative who got in touch with an officer who was able somehow to erase the record of the arrests and imprisonments. "Later I would wonder," he said, "whether they had really been erased or only temporarily put on hold."

At first he stayed in Erzincan, where his fiancée and her family were living. During his time off he would sit in coffee shops and watch the card and backgammon games. He had an affair with a woman for the first time when he went to a public house where prostitutes were working legally. In 1985 he broke up with his fiancée after harsh words were spoken. It had turned out to be a tense, uneasy alliance because there was a divide financially between her family and his. At the same time—and perhaps this is a key reason—Suleyman had become interested in a second cousin, Sukran. Her parents were fond of Suleyman, and so too, it seems, was Sukran, who soon developed thoughts of marriage. "At the beginning she was shy," Suleyman said. "One day we were caught while kissing by her younger brother. We felt extremely ashamed. Sukran begged her brother not to tell her parents."

It was around this time that another woman, Nurhan, also came into the picture. Suleyman and a friend were organizing tours to visit the tomb of an Alevi saint in the town of Haci Bektas in the Nevşehir province. During one of these trips their bus picked up a young girl and her mother. It was a case of immediate attraction. Suleyman noticed the young girl looking at him as soon as she got on the bus—"as if we knew each other." He liked the way she looked, too. "After we arrived at the tomb," Suleyman said, "a folk singer who was with us sang some Alevi songs. We formed a circle in an open field while some of our friends were preparing the meal which consisted of bulgur and meat." They participated in the Alevi cem ceremony and in a ritual that involved people trying symbolically to go through "the hole in the rock." As the belief goes, "If you have no sins, you are lighter and can go through the hole in the rock. Nurhan was a little heavier and she had difficulty making it through!"

Suleyman told me about how the two of them "tied colourful ribbons to a wish tree." As he recalled it: "I was amazed at the mull tree, which stays green throughout the year. While preparing the barbeque Nurhan put salt on meat as a way of showing how much she loved me. She told me that she had a son but that she and her husband were separated and she was going to get a divorce. I kissed her for a long time and passionately as we sat on a rock just near the water. Nurhan told me she prayed at the tomb of the saint so that we could marry. The poor woman's prayer did not come true. I still have a lot of respect for her pure love."

In that same year the brother of Suleyman's fiancée contacted the deputy chair of the Turkish Grand Assembly, who in turn provided a letter to the director of the Turkish National Railways. As a result Suleyman was able to get a good job as an engineer with the national railway system. For almost six years he would spend his time making sure the citizens of Turkey were transported safely around the country.

Throughout this time, as he worked on the railways, Suleyman was involved with a number of women, but he was not ready to put down roots. His experiences of torture and imprisonment had left him deeply unsettled, unsure of his future. He became interested in another Alevi girl, a day-care teacher, and his friends tried to match him up with relatives. He also met a Turkish girl during a course. She was a Sunni, and her family told him that he was not acceptable because he was an Alevi Kurd.

His career as an engineer was progressing. After a year working in the city of Sivas he was promoted and transferred to Ankara, "the heart of Turkey." After he got to know the city, he would go often to the Chamber of Electrical Engineers (not to the Chamber of the Mechanical Engineers, which was controlled by a right-wing group). At the Chamber, "a kind of club," he found other men who were either technologists or engineers. They often talked about the soccer teams and other sports—and rarely mentioned politics. He would read leftist magazines and newspapers and attend meetings and seminars. Things had eased up a little in Turkey, and these activities did not seem as dangerous as they once were.

In the meantime Suleyman's family had been forced by events to uproot themselves, leaving Dersim to go once again to the town of Bursa in the northwest part of the country. This time the trouble had started with left-wing militants rather than right-wing Turkish extremists.

In 1985 a radical left-wing Turkish group was operating in the area of Dersim. The group, known by the acronym TIKKO, was hard-line communist and espoused violence as a means of implementing an extreme nationalist vision for the Kurdish people.[9] That year the Turkish paramilitary ambushed and killed some members of TIKKO as they made their way through the forests of Dersim. The army had clearly known that the TIKKO militants were coming and had trapped them in the forest.

The members of TIKKO in the area accused Suleyman's father of betraying them. Frightened once again, the Goven family moved west and out of the reach of TIKKO, or so they thought.

By that time, Suleyman had grown more compassionate about the fear that held his father in its grip, the fear of violent leftists. Suleyman would send him money and make more of an effort to draw him out. His father seemed pleased with this attention.

One night in the summer of 1990 Suleyman had a dream, one of many dreams of a foreboding kind. "I saw a fireplace but no fire. The fire had gone out and my mother was very sad." Around the same time he received a phone call at work asking him to return home immediately. When he got home, he said, "I walked towards the house and saw the religious men washing the body of my father in the backyard. I took his hand and bent down to kiss it . . ."

Throughout his diaries Suleyman always makes note of this day: July 29. It remains a time of tears. Twice a year for some time he sent memorial announcements to Kurdish newspapers about an innocent man who was murdered by leftist extremists. It bothered Suleyman then, and it bothers him now, that his father, an innocent man, was accused and left without any way of defending himself. The son remembers this, again and again.

Suleyman's mother and father had been eating supper with the two youngest boys. It was the end of the Alevi twelve-day fast, a special meal and a special time. The TIKKO squad burst in and shot Suleyman's father.

After the shooting the TIKKO squad released an announcement in the media stating that the father had been an informant. Suleyman had no reason to believe this accusation. He did know that a cousin of his mother was captured by a TIKKO group. The cousin was tortured—a piece of wood had been hammered down his mouth until he died. Suleyman wondered what this cousin was forced to say before he died.

Suleyman responded immediately, calling a press conference of his own to denounce the actions of TIKKO. The denunciation was reported in the national newspaper and by various radio and TV stations. Suleyman knew there would be consequences and that TIKKO would try to silence him.

It was the second time he had gone to the media that summer. He was becoming ever more visible, vulnerable. The first time came after the administration of the Turkish railways had decided to give more pay only to engineers who had graduated from certain universities. It was an issue of professional discrimination, and Suleyman and a friend decided to challenge the decision in an administrative court. They met with great resistance from the engineers who belonged to the MHP, faculty members who were mostly in other departments; but they were able to convince most of the engineers in their department, and Suleyman took the case to the media.

The director general of the railways began making inquiries about the people who were taking the issue to the public. Suleyman's records opened up on the past and he was taken to police headquarters, detained once again, tortured again, and released again.

That year Suleyman was planning to get engaged to Sukran, his second cousin. But it became clear that he could not stay in Turkey. She begged him to promise to marry her, but he felt unable to make this commitment. Later he said, "If I made such a commitment I would feel guilty until the end of my life."

The train began to leave the station of Turkey.

It chugged along the line of long suffering.

You cannot stay.
You cannot stay.
You cannot stay.

• • •

In mid-December 1990 Suleyman fled Turkey and journeyed through Bulgaria and Yugoslavia to Switzerland, France, and the Netherlands, and finally to Germany and his visit with Nurhan. He did not find his answer to life there. "I really liked her and she wanted to marry me, but I didn't want to take advantage of her to stay in Germany. She had filed for a divorce but it hadn't come through and there was a child." He stayed at a motel and visited Nurhan at a school where she was working as a cleaner. He found the place, and the life, confusing—he would try to get directions from people and it seemed they often gave him the wrong directions. Or maybe he just didn't understand. "I could see the way they looked at me and I did not feel comfortable." From Germany he went to Sweden. He thought he could perhaps make a refugee claim in Sweden, but the Kurdish people he met there warned him about close contacts between the Swedish and Turkish intelligence services. He was able to get on a plane to Ireland, arriving in Dublin on Christmas Day. He had been travelling for three months.

In Ireland he loved the lighthearted quality of the music he heard in the pubs. "It is such a nice, joyful dance music. It reminds me of the beauty of Ireland and the beautiful girls and the sounds of the sea. The music is very amazing and is from an old tradition." But he realized that it could take a very long time for his refugee claim to be heard, and there were few if any translators he could

count on to help. He thought of going to Australia, but met a pleasant and friendly Canadian man in a hostel and that made him change
his mind. He flew to Heathrow to get a flight to Canada but was
turned back. The officials there said he needed a visa for Canada.

Returning to Dublin, he went to the Canadian embassy to try to
obtain a visa. Later he told me: "I said I wanted to study. The officer
asked me some questions but I think he knew what I was trying to
do. He asked me what I was doing in Ireland. I lied and said I was
studying at a college. He phoned the college and no one answered.
After a half an hour he stamped my papers. He had said he had
worked in Turkey and was aware of the situation for Kurds and
Armenians."

On April 8, 1991, Suleyman Goven, the man who would be
tagged a terrorist, arrived in Toronto at Pearson Airport. We would
meet when the sound of the train again appeared out of the past,
with its rumbling notice.

You cannot stay.

You cannot stay.

You cannot stay.

THE FACELESS ONE

DOGS HOWL. Wolves howl. And so do human beings when they are struggling with nameless ones, faceless ones, all night in the dark.

Slowly I began to understand why Suleyman had howled after his interview with the Canadian Security and Intelligence Services. They had asked him to betray his fellow Kurds, just as the Turkish security services had asked him to inform on others when he was tortured. The Canadians had accused him of being a terrorist just as the Turks had accused him of similar deeds. The Canadians had interrogated him. He knew he was innocent, just as his father had been innocent in Turkey. He suspected that he had been betrayed by other Kurds in Canada.

The deepening crisis for Suleyman was that although he had learned that innocence counted for little in Turkey—it had not counted for his father, and it had not counted for himself—he now began to wonder if things would be any different in Canada. He had believed that justice and due process mattered here, and now he was not so sure. "If the intelligence service decides that I am a member of a terrorist group because I tried to set up the Kurdish centre and took part in demonstrations for our people," he told me, "then we have to question the democracy of this country."

He began to call the CSIS agents the "uncles," a term used in Turkey to describe the security forces, and he referred to government bureaucrats as "the gangs."

In the months following the interview with the two CSIS agents he flailed around, yelling at anyone who happened to be nearby. He felt trapped, powerless. When I met up with him over those days, his anger frightened me at times. Some refugee lawyers and staff at non-governmental organizations such as Amnesty International told stories of how he blasted them about the dirty rotten system and how they were not doing enough to help him. Your day will come, they said. I was sure it would, someday soon.

I was also sure that something could be done. I was convinced that some terrible mistake had been made. Or had it?

I took his side, and still I wondered. That long trip through Europe? An engineer? An army officer? The CSIS questions did not completely leave my mind. When I went over to the Kurdish Community Centre I found myself watching him closely, looking for signs of threat and violence. I listened to what the other Kurds were saying. I listened extra-carefully when he translated for other Kurds. Was he interpolating? Was he telling them what to say on their refugee papers?

The question about his possible involvement in the Kurdistan Workers' Party troubled me, and I did some research on the organization. It had been born in reaction to the destruction of Kurdish lands in the eastern part of Turkey and had opted for a military solution to the problem. The PKK had been able to attract some fierce fighters from the villages. It trained them in camps in Syria. As a disciplined force, employing guerrilla tactics, the PKK had been able to wreak havoc on Turkish forces in the east. It had also instilled a sense of pride among Kurds, even those who did not agree with its methods, because as an organization it was doing more than just lamenting the atrocities committed against the Kurds. Still, some PKK groups were killing innocent civilians. Others tried to inflict damage on the national economy by destabilizing the tourism industry, capturing tourists and bombing areas that tour groups travelled through. In Europe the PKK had reportedly bombed or damaged various buildings associated with the Turkish government or businesses.[1]

As I saw it, there were freedom fighters and there were terrorists. The question was whether Suleyman was a freedom fighter or a terrorist, or both?

And that howl, was it the howl of a dog or a wolf?

I listened to hear what resounded in my mind and my soul. I could not afford to be wrong, of this I was sure.

I took my point of reference from what I knew to be true. Here was an intelligent and gifted young man who needed only four more courses in Canada to become a qualified engineer. But he would not be able to take those courses until he received his landed immigrant papers. Whether or not he got that landed status would depend on the result of his security review.

To be accepted as landed immigrants, refugees must pass a medical examination, a police check to ensure that they have not committed crimes in Canada, and a security check to make sure that they do not constitute a threat to national security. Without the landed immigrant papers, Suleyman would have to pay foreign student fees; he would not be eligible for a student loan. His life and his studies were on hold, and I wondered how long he could hold on.

The days and months passed and Suleyman had no word from the authorities about his application for landed immigrant status. Through these months after that seemingly endless day in October I phoned around trying to find out the reason for the delay. I learned that security checks should never take longer than two years—and two years had already passed. Finally I was able to find out that CSIS had sent its recommendation to Immigration on August 30, 1995, some ten months after the interrogation.

Silence.

I asked one of our volunteers at Romero House to use an Access to Information and Privacy Request to find out what was happening. The request process is supposed to take thirty days, but it was more than a year before we received Suleyman Goven's file from Immigration Canada. Half of it was blacked out; the rest said nothing. There was no indication as to what the problem was.

Nevertheless, the sight of those blacked-out sections startled me. I wondered if they knew something that I did not. Could I say that I really knew Suleyman Goven?

In February 1996 Suleyman was again elected president of the Kurdish Centre. He was the almost unanimous choice of the community. Once again he had been summoned to lead, and he said he felt "blessed" by this honour. He would remain loyal to them. He pledged to promote their best interests. But things in the Kurdish community were getting murky. The community was coming under increasing scrutiny from CSIS. The uncles were making visits to Kurds in their homes, and from the agents' questions it was clear that they thought the Centre might be a front for the PKK. Agents were visiting the Kurdish Centre and asking people about its activities and its president. The uncles were present at the Newroz, a New Year's event.

The sense of threat was vague but all-pervasive. People became unsure of themselves and each other. The agents moved in and out of the Kurdish community, nameless people who came and went; yet their power was enormous. Everyone knew this. People worried about their phone calls. They worried about the uncles with cameras who began appearing at their social events. They worried about each other. Conversations became strained and guarded. The community began to fracture and divide, and some people dropped away from the Centre. There was a growing suspicion that CSIS was recruiting spies from within the community. After his election as president Suleyman knew that he had a dangerous rival in the figure of a shadowy man whom we shall call H. People were suspicious of a Canadian woman who had insinuated herself into the events of the Kurdish community and begun a relationship with H.[2] There was a break-in at Suleyman's apartment. Along with precious mementoes that he had brought from Turkey the thieves also took some important documents, including a copy of the newspaper article in which he had denounced the violent tactics of TIKKO.

Eventually it became clear to Suleyman that his leadership in the Centre might be holding up his security clearance. He quit the Centre in 1997, and the following year H. moved in to become the new leader.

• • •

There was another fragment of truth I could hold onto. I knew what I had heard during that endless interview on that endless day in October. Regardless of my questions about who Suleyman was or what he might have done in his life, it was clear to me that what had happened at that interrogation was wrong.

I was in the process of writing a book, *At the Border Called Hope: Where Refugees Are Neighbours.* I decided to include a description of the interview I had attended with Suleyman. When the book appeared in January 1997, it was read by an unusual array of people. Even today I hear from people for whom the book was a revelation—of the complex reality of the lives of refugees, both funny and sad moments—and of the underside of the immigration system.

One day that spring I received a phone call from Sylvia MacKenzie, a lawyer in Ottawa. She said that she worked for the Security Intelligence Review Committee (SIRC) and had read my book. She suggested that we meet for breakfast in Toronto. She explained that SIRC was supposed to be the watchdog over the activities of CSIS. It had been set up as an independent body that reports to the Parliament of Canada. I was intrigued, to say the least.

We met for breakfast in the café of one of the downtown hotels. I was surprised to meet a charming and lovely younger woman. Sylvia was a delightful person, discreet and obviously competent. She wanted to talk about my book.

"Is it true what you said about the interview with Suleyman Goven?"

"Yes," I answered. "It's true, unfortunately."

"Are you sure?"

"Yes, I am. I took notes most of the way through. I wrote them up right away. I know what I heard. They propositioned him, offering landed papers if he would become a spy on his own community."

"That's completely unacceptable if it's true."

Sylvia told me how to launch a complaint against CSIS. She suggested that I could do it as a witness to the "interrogation." It would be a rather long process, she said. First a complaint had to be made to the director of CSIS. If his reply was not satisfactory, the process could move over to SIRC.

After the meeting with Sylvia I phoned Suleyman and we met to discuss the possibility of lodging a complaint against CSIS. Given that we had found out so little from the Access to Information request, he was pleased with the possibility. It would be a chance to find out who his accusers were and what he had been accused of. In that long interrogation we had come into all-too-close contact with two of the agents, but who were the nameless, faceless ones who were blocking Suleyman's application for landed immigrant status?

I was a little more hesitant. I was not used to dealing with secret services. They were not the kind of people I wanted to deal with. Yet I knew this was the right thing to do. The way ahead was not clear, but the road had closed behind us.

Suleyman and I drafted the complaint together, focusing on the length of the security determination and how it had been conducted.

The complaint was accepted, and a SIRC review was scheduled to begin in September 1998. That process would grind its way forward through autumn and winter and into the spring of 1999. During that time, though, I also attended another security hearing with a different Kurd. The CSIS agent conducting the interview tried to keep me out of the interview and was about to firmly close the door in my face, but I managed to block his effort by wedging my foot in the door. I insisted that the refugee had a right to have someone with him. By that time, most of the Kurdish refugees were terrified by the security interviews, by what they might be asked to do.

During the interview I witnessed the same thing all over again. The refugee was told: *if you help us understand the Kurdish community, we will give you your papers.* The message this time might have been a little more subtle, but it was clear.

After that interview I began to take closer notice of the results of the Kurdish security interviews. I noticed, for example, that some Kurds were getting their landed immigrant papers within three months of applying, while the requests of others were being held in abeyance for years.

The painful truth dawned on me: some Kurds were accepting the CSIS offer and others were not. I remember one Kurdish man who had come to me before his security interview. He was desperately worried about his wife and child, who were in an extremely dangerous situation after the Gulf War. Was there something I could do? I told him that I probably could not intervene for about a year and a half after he made his application for landed immigrant status—that this was the normal period of time for the checks to be made.

Some three months after I had spoken with this man, I heard that his wife and child had arrived on the basis of his application to sponsor them. I realized that he had probably made a deal. I did not want to judge him. None of us know what is really going on or the kinds of pressure that can be brought to bear on a person. From time to time I see this man at the subway station. He seems embarrassed to see me. I find it hard to smile, but I try to say hello.

The wolves were circling.

I became less concerned about Suleyman and more terrified by these secret agents who were supposed to be protecting innocent people. The agents of the Canadian state were using the tactic employed by the agents of the Turkish state—dividing the Kurds from one another, terrifying them into submission.

I started to speak with other refugees in the Kurdish community, and the conversations confirmed my suspicions: that CSIS was propositioning almost every refugee to work against the others. And more: I learned that the CSIS agents were specifically asking them to inform on Suleyman, to sign statements indicating that Suleyman was a member of the PKK.

I asked the various refugees to organize a meeting, and a number of them had the courage to attend. In all, fourteen Kurdish refugees were willing to state publicly that they had been asked to spy in return for getting landed status in Canada. Their stories were particular, and painful. For instance, one man and his wife had arrived in Canada seven years before. They had been forced to leave abruptly, leaving behind, with their family in Turkey, a two-year-old son. He was now nine, and no longer recognized them as his parents. Whenever they phoned him in Turkey to tell him that they loved him, he called them liars. They were in agony about this. Another man who arrived in 1991 had been forced to leave behind his wife and two daughters (one was six and a half months old; the other was three). He was suffering from this forced separation, and his family was no longer safe in Turkey. I talked to two other men who had been engaged before they left Turkey. Because of the delays in sending for their fiancées, the women back home thought they were lying and had broken off the engagements.

On April 19, 1998, fourteen Kurdish men, including Suleyman, signed a joint statement:

> We hoped to seek refuge and find a peaceful life in Canada. We were all successful at our immigration hearings. . . . It seemed as though everything was progressing in a natural manner; however, when CSIS started conducting security checks, we became

subject to the same post-traumatic stress that we had already endured in Turkey. During our security checks, CSIS agents made threats with regard to our receiving our landed papers. CSIS harassed, intimidated, and abused us for not cooperating with them. The cooperation they sought was for us to inform on fellow Kurds. These practices put all of us under great pressure, which we refer to as our post-traumatic stress. Without landed status, our lives are in limbo in Canada. Living in limbo is tantamount to having a Damocles sword hanging over our heads: We encounter restrictions in our ability to undertake studies as we cannot obtain student loans; to travel as we cannot leave and enter Canada freely, and even to obtain credit cards . . .

We all have all known great suffering and constant sorrow. As people who were oppressed and persecuted by Turks in the past, we do not want to be harassed, intimidated and abused by the Canadian Immigration system and CSIS in the present. The Canadian government has turned a blind eye to this situation because of trade relations with Turkey.

The statement ends with a plea: "We humbly implore you to bring our concerns to the attention of the Canadian government and to other international bodies as we are feeling desperate and as though we are in a prison with no walls."

Through this time the Sanctuary Coalition was meeting steadily and had become increasingly involved in the case of Suleyman and the other Kurdish refugees. Michael Creal, the chair of the Coalition, was outraged by the blatant injustice that the Kurds were being subjected to. He had begun to take Suleyman to heart. So too had

Andrew Brouwer, a newer member of the Coalition. Andrew was working at Citizens for Public Justice before going on to study law part-time at the University of Toronto. He also worked as a researcher for the Maytree Foundation, an organization dedicated to reducing poverty and inequality in Canada and to building vibrant civic communities—work that includes a strong commitment to immigrants and refugees. The members of the Coalition did not think that the Kurds who were in limbo needed to be offered protection in a church, at least not yet, but did believe they needed the support of the mainline churches. Michael Creal and the other members of the Coalition had already been around the block with Immigration Canada, several times. We knew how intractable bureaucracies could be.

We also recognized how difficult it was for politicians to truly shape the departments for which they were responsible. Nevertheless, we decided to go to Parliament to publicize the terrible predicament of the Kurdish refugees in the face of this intimidation. We had come to see that refugees live within a virtual apartheid system in the country, under a different set of laws, with almost no protection against the nameless, faceless security apparatus.

We also decided to go public with the statement of the fourteen Kurds and spoke specifically to Allan Thompson of the *Toronto Star*. Thompson then did an article relating the statement of the Kurds, and in the process conducted what he called a "rare media interview" with the director of csis, Ward Elcock. The director's response was evasive and unclear, to say the least. According to Thompson, Elcock stated that it was "not his agency's policy to entice refugees to work as informants in exchange for help in getting status in Canada." But the director of csis also "refused to confirm or deny allegations that csis uses its sway with the immigration department as a tool in its efforts to extract information from refugees and refugee claimants." Elcock did reportedly state: "It's clear in policy that investigators, when they are trying to recruit somebody, cannot promise assistance with status and that anything that people offer to us is voluntary."[3]

Andrew Brouwer arranged our visit to Parliament Hill, and I drove to Ottawa with Suleyman and another Kurdish man who was living in suspended animation because of delays with his security clearance. We stayed at my sister's house in Ottawa, and it was then that I realized how "single" these guys had become. They grazed through the refrigerator and sat watching the television while my sister and I prepared a meal and set the table. I could see that they had become accustomed to eating alone, living alone, feeling alone.

We left for Parliament Hill on the morning of Tuesday, April 21, 1998, and visited with several members of the Standing Committee on Immigration and Citizenship. After that we attended a luncheon meeting with Liberal MPs from the Toronto area. Later in the afternoon the three of us testified before the House of Commons committee. I described what had happened on that day in October 1994 and how many Kurds, probably more than I knew, were being propositioned by csis. Suleyman made an impassioned plea that he be allowed to get on with his life.

Most of the parliamentarians we talked to frankly expressed their intense dissatisfaction with the Immigration Department. Each of the Toronto-area MPs had been forced to hire a staff person to handle Immigration files almost full-time because of the number of situations that were falling through the cracks in the system.

After our testimony before the committee, several members stated their outrage that refugees should be placed in this untenable and immoral situation. Liberals John McKay and Steve Mahoney and Bloc Québécois member Raymonde Folco were appalled by the news that Kurds were being asked to spy in exchange for landed status. McKay in particular said he was fed up with the gobbledy-gook from Immigration. A member of Parliament from Montreal made a special point of questioning the influence of the Turkish government on the situation of Kurds in Canada.

A few days after our visit, the Immigration Minister, Lucienne Robillard, said that she would ask the Solicitor General to look into the allegations against csis. "They shouldn't use any threat to the newcomers to our country," Robillard said. "They are seeking protection from our country, so they are vulnerable people."[4]

One of the most interesting comments to surface as a result of our visit to Parliament Hill came from Stan Dromisky, the Liberal Party MP for Thunder Bay–Atikokan. Dromisky was the chair of the Standing Committee on Immigration and Citizenship, and during our visit to his office he told us that he would speak to the Minister about our concerns. Later, in a phone conversation, Dromisky said to Andrew Brouwer, "If you want my advice, you should lay off the criticism of Turkey."

The penny dropped. The Kurdish refugees had already figured this out, long ago, but neither Andrew nor I had focused on this aspect of the issue. We had not carefully considered how the csis attitude to the Kurdish refugees might just have a lot do to with the reality of Turkey and its connections with Canada.

• • •

When I returned from Ottawa I dusted off my journalistic and research skills and began to dig into this possibility. I started by noting that Dromisky was the president of the Canada-Turkish Friendship Society and had recently travelled to Turkey. I found that Canada was involved in serious trade negotiations with Turkey. Against the objections of many environmental groups Canada was pushing to sell CANDU reactors to Turkey. Over the objections of the Canadian Taxpayers Federation, the government was willing to loan millions of dollars to Turkey to help the country make the purchase.[5] Much of the concern, in Canada and throughout the world, had to do with the plan for the reactors to be located in the Akkuyu area, an earthquake zone.

By 1998 Turkey had been in the final stages of considering the possibility of nuclear reactors as a solution to its energy shortage. The Atomic Energy of Canada Limited, with its CANDU reactor, was one of three companies involved in intense bidding for the project. Canada was also eagerly trying to sell CF-5 fighter airplanes to Turkey and had already committed itself to a large sale of military equipment. Over a period of four years, according to researcher Richard Sanders of the Coalition to Oppose the Arms Trade, "The Department of Foreign Affairs has approved military export permits to Turkey totalling $26 million. Our exports have included small and large calibre weapons, computer systems for targeting and firing weapons, military vehicles, toxicological agents and tear gas, aircraft and helicopters and a plethora of electronic equipment for military use."[6] Some of this equipment would surely be used to subdue any unrest in the Kurdish areas of the country. Human rights groups throughout the world had condemned the sale of any military equipment to Turkey. The country's record of human rights abuses was widely known and well documented. In response to these criticisms Turkey had argued that it was simply dealing with Kurdish terrorists such as the PKK.

Several companies, notably in Quebec, had negotiated important commercial deals with Turkey: Bombardier Aerospace, SNC-
Lavalin, BC Gas, Nortel. One of the greatest ironies is that many of
the Bombardier contracts had to do with light-rail transit in cities
such as Ankara and Adana. If life had not picked up Suleyman and
cast him away from his country, he might well have been working
on one of those railways.

One incident in particular indicates the extent to which trade
considerations with Turkey could trump human rights considerations on the part of the Canadian government. In 1998 the City of
Montreal decided to build a monument to the countless victims of
the Armenian genocide. Montreal has a significant Armenian community, and the city was poised to approve the monument in a public park. The mayor of Montreal indicated that the federal Minister
of International Trade had contacted him to say that erecting this
monument would offend the Turkish government and would affect
the contracts of two companies in Montreal. The plans for the
monuments were put on hold. Clearly, trade with Turkey was taking precedence over the human rights of Armenians and their legitimate cultural and political expression.[7]

In response to this controversy, Dromisky issued a statement
casting doubt on the size and magnitude of the Armenian genocide. The Minister of State for Foreign Affairs said in the House
of Commons that what happened to the Armenians might be more
in the nature of a "tragic event" than a matter of genocide. The Minister of International Trade, Jim Peterson, suggested that every
effort had been made to discreetly raise issues of human rights with
the Turkish government.

It was becoming clearer to me: many of the assumptions held
by Canadian officials about Kurdish refugees had most likely been

shaped by the government of Turkey—the very government that had forced the Kurds to leave their country.

The howling of the wolves was echoing far away in Canada.

• • •

In the minds of many Western governments, Canada included, there were good Kurds and bad Kurds. The good Kurds were those who opposed the Iraqi and Iranian regimes: the enemy of my enemy is my friend. The bad Kurds were those who opposed my friend, the regime in Turkey: the enemy of my friend is my enemy.

Learning about the extent of Turkish influence on the situation of Kurds in Canada was useful but distressing. The impoverished little Kurdish community was up against powerful interests as well as a vast indifference.

One Sunday afternoon I had a visit from a married couple who had emigrated from Turkey and were looking for help with housing. They were not Kurdish, and the man had been a major in the Turkish army. He had been in charge of military units in the eastern part of the country. I did not say anything about my increasing involvement and interest in that part of the world. After telling me that he had not mentioned to anyone that he had been in the Turkish army, he added: "You know, everything people say about what the Turkish army is doing to the Kurds is true, especially in the east. The killings, the rape and torture. I couldn't stand it anymore."

During this time Suleyman was alternately in low spirits and full of purpose. He was on antidepressants, trying to fight off the wolves inside. He seemed unable to focus on his future—which was hardly surprising because that future was so uncertain. The government was making increasing use of "security certificates"—a process established under the Immigration and Refugee Protection Act aimed at "the removal from Canada of non-Canadians who have no legal right to be here and who pose a serious threat to Canada and Canadians."[8] Under a security certificate, authorities could pick up refugees and detain them indefinitely, without charging them or letting them know the basis for the charges. Suleyman was working full-time as a translator for various immigration lawyers, helping Kurdish refugees and Turkish dissidents. Some of the lawyers he worked for told him that he could be picked up at any moment. "When they think someone is an enemy, that justifies all forms of mistreatment," he said. "It is not important to them that you have been a victim of torture. I stood up against an oppressive regime in my country and for this I was tortured." In his new country, it seemed to Suleyman, he was also being tortured, this time not physically but mentally.

Suleyman seemed to have abandoned his dream of going to university. He now spent most of his days at The Forum restaurant at St. Clair and Dufferin streets. He would sit at the same table all day, drinking coffee and helping new arrivals with the procedures and papers that they did not understand. The Forum had become his office, and we knew we could find him there most times of the day or night. He did not look well. The dark circles under his eyes had widened. He was irritable. I wondered when he slept, if he slept. "This is not different from what happened to me in Turkey," he said to me. "I feel like I am living in an open prison. The police are like a lying machine. If they thought I was a member of a terrorist group, why don't they deport me?" He said his inner peace was "being destroyed from the outside, and it's difficult to establish your inner peace."

He raged against the "motherfucking uncles" and the gangs, and I now recognized the roar as the sound of fragility. "The bureaucrats always carry out their owner's wishes and claim they are acting according to regulations, but they are robots who make the system work. They don't see refugees as human beings." He talked about how the security officers were "small cogs" within a machine. They were forgetting about the values of humanity, and becoming like wild animals. "If those who are oppressed and who have suffered don't have enough moral support, they will be crushed by the system and those individuals." The refugees who were subject to this process were also in danger of losing their values, of beginning "to doubt they are human." The "cruel system" was aiming at making people submissive.

As the days went on, the slightest thing would set Suleyman off. One evening he wrote in his diary:

> This morning we went to the courtroom and found out that the hearing was postponed. The lawyer knew, but he didn't tell me. I had coffee in a restaurant nearby. When my coffee and toast was late, I yelled at the waitress. I said this is a kind of psychology and you express your anger. It has nothing to do with the girls. My anger also spoils other people's inner peace.

In an effort to help him to at least keep his own life on track, I said that if he really wanted to go to university I would find him the money to do so—the extra money needed to pay the foreign student fees. He never did follow up on this suggestion. He seemed unable to settle down in his personal life. He had become involved with several women, enjoyed their company. Occasionally he would shyly bring a girl over to Romero House and introduce her to me. And then a few months later he would say it was over. In the end he was not able to make any commitment to a woman, or to himself. Despite his past record of engagements and near-marriage, he was now not able to think in terms of a wife and family.

He began to think of himself as someone who was "depending on grief." He thought a lot about death. He wrote that he was "afraid of death." He wondered whether it was because he was now middle-aged, whether it was a reality he would have to accept. "There will be an inevitable end. Even the richest, most brutal, most powerful, most intelligent people have not been able to change this reality, so it must be one of the most natural things for me as an ordinary person." His mind turned to thoughts of the dead members of his family, especially his father and his sister. He recorded going out for a walk one evening and thinking of them, trying somehow to communicate. "My father's soul was around me. I believe that there is a communication with the souls, there is a bridge between those who died and the real world. I don't know why nowadays I just keep thinking about death."

On some days he felt almost trapped. He continued to try to help refugees from Turkey, whether Kurdish or Turkish. When he took them to the Immigration office, someone asked him whether he was getting money for this, whether he was a smuggler of human beings. A female officer asked about how he got involved with these people. He told her that he was well known in the Turkish and Kurdish communities. "After seven hours we left the Immigration office and I took a deep breath. If you try to help people, then they try to accuse you of being a smuggler. If you don't help them, then they get lost, these poor people get lost."

One day while we were having yet another cup of coffee at The Forum, I looked at this raggedy man who seemed to be aging as we talked. And I thought: *A terrorist would have done something violent by now; a terrorist would have left by now. He is not a terrorist.*

THE NAMELESS ONE

I N 1998 Suleyman's life became focused on the SIRC review, scheduled to begin in September. He began to assemble a legal team, a process that required good judgment. Several "fashion lawyers" had offered to take on his complaint because they knew it had already drawn a considerable amount of attention in the media. In the end he decided to approach Barbara Jackman, who had justifiably earned a reputation as being one of the finest refugee lawyers in the country. She had become known as someone who could find precedents from areas of the law far removed from immigration and apply them in creative ways. Instead of turning this ability and reputation into a completely profit-oriented practice, she had the unusual tendency of taking on cases in which the client had little or no ability to pay. She worked out of a hole in the wall and was anything but a "fashion lawyer."

Sharryn Aiken became the second member of Suleyman's legal team. Sharry had been involved with Kurdish refugee claims during time spent at the Refugee Law Office in Toronto, and she was aware of how the community was being subjected to harsh discrimination, or worse. She carried these concerns forward during her term as the eloquent president of the Canadian Council for Refugees. Intelligent and clear, Sharry would anchor the presentation of Suleyman's complaint.

For Suleyman, the official complaint against CSIS was a new dimension of his struggle. "If we didn't make this complaint, this gang might have arrested me. I'm happy and proud of myself that we made this decision." He was convinced that he and his thirteen friends were acting in an honourable way. "I know I cannot bring back eight lost years," he wrote, but on the other hand: "Either you live as an honourable man or as a dishonourable one and your life ends like this." He had not capitulated to the Turkish military's fascist coup in 1980, and he was not now going to surrender himself to any institution in Canada. "Nobody can change me or make me surrender."

• • •

On September 15, 1998, I took the subway east and south to the centre of the city to attend the first session of the hearing of the Security Intelligence Review Committee into the case of Suleyman Goven. As the person who had officially filed the complaint, I was committed to attending all the sessions, which would eventually spread out over a six-month period. That day, as I sat in the subway car, I wondered what they would look like, these previously nameless, faceless entities who held such power over the lives of others. I had seen plenty of Suleyman and other members of the Kurdish community, but I had not really faced "the uncles" except for that one tedious day in October 1994. I expected to be impressed. I was in for a big surprise.

I got out at Dundas and Yonge and walked south to the little church that had clung stubbornly to its location behind the Eaton Centre—and to its convictions in the midst of the surrounding commercial sprawl in the very heart of the city. The Church of the Holy Trinity had anchored the Sanctuary Coalition throughout Suleyman's long struggle, and now the members wanted to gather with Suleyman in prayer before the first session began. We offered a blessing for Suleyman, the blessing of security. At the end of the service, we gave him a stone to carry, a touchstone, a reminder that he was not alone. We also prayed for ourselves, I think. It had been an exhausting struggle and futile thus far. We wanted it to end.

The SIRC hearings were to be held nearby, in the boardroom of a large law firm in the office tower of the Eaton Centre. The chair of the hearings, the Honourable Robert Keith Rae, was a senior partner in the firm. Bob Rae's assignment to chair the complaint was an encouragement for us, not just because we were familiar, and for the most part comfortable, with his political views, but also because he had a reputation for intelligence and fairness. He had been the leader of the New Democratic Party in Ontario and provincial premier from 1990 to 1995. After he lost the 1995 election he had returned to the practice of law, and he was now spending a great deal of time working as a mediator of various social issues.

I walked with Suleyman over to the Eaton Centre and we took the elevator up to the eighth floor of the office tower. We met Suleyman's lawyers in the lobby of the law firm. They were ready to go. We were ushered into the boardroom, which looked a bit like a newsroom. The proceedings were being recorded, and microphones, tape recorders, and electrical cords were all over the place. Our group sat down on one side of a long wooden table and faced the people who would decide Suleyman's fate, or so we thought at that time.

Bob Rae was already established on one side of the table, in the centre, and to his left were two lawyers from the Justice Department who were representing csis. To his right were Sylvia MacKenzie and a lawyer contracted to represent sirc. We would spend almost fifteen full days together over the next six months.

Various witnesses were summoned to appear before the chair of the review. Suleyman and I were allowed to be present during most of their testimony—most, but not all. We were able to see the faces of most of the csis officers who had been directly involved in the assessment that he was a terrorist. We learned their names, we saw what they wore, and we heard how they talked. However, neither Suleyman and I nor the lawyers representing our complaint were able to be present when these officers were questioned in camera or *ex parte*. These were the really secret sessions that presumably involved national security—the sessions that probably involved naming names. Rae, as chair, was present during all of the in camera sessions, and we were provided with summaries of those sessions. But this approach meant that Suleyman would never know exactly what he was being accused of, or why, and by whom.

It was like wrestling in the dark with something, someone, no one and everyone.

In the hearings themselves, Rae set the tone at the outset. He said he wanted to run the process in a dignified manner and would ensure that the complainants and members of the service would be treated with equal respect. He also established that the entire complaint process was secret and that the evidence presented could not be made public.[1]

In the evidence disclosed prior to this first session, we had learned that csis had sent its "recommendation" to the Immigration

Department in August 1995. That document indicated that CSIS could not recommend a security certificate or deportation *at this time*; it could also not recommend that Suleyman receive landed immigrant status. In fact, it recommended nothing. It suggested everything.

In essence the CSIS case against Suleyman went along these lines:

> *The Kurdish Information Centre is a front for the PKK, and Suleyman Goven was a founder and president of the Centre.*
> *The PKK is a terrorist group.*
> *Suleyman Goven has admitted that he is a member of the PKK.*
> *Therefore Suleyman Goven is a terrorist.*

The first witness for CSIS was to be its expert on terrorism. I am not sure what I was expecting, but perhaps I had seen too many James Bond movies. I expected to be impressed by our country's professional agents. There was still an outside chance, I thought, that they really did have something on Suleyman.

"The expert" came in and rather quickly acknowledged that he was "knowledgeable" but not really an expert. His specialty, he said at the outset, was the kind of information that could be found in "open sources" or journals, books, and newspapers. This knowledgeable person was a slightly rotund, somewhat balding man with a bow tie. He presented his curriculum vitae, which the lawyers for CSIS underlined: he had written an important book on terrorism, and had authored several articles on the subject as well.

The knowledgeable man began by giving a sweeping view of the dangers of terrorism in the world. I was almost ready to get swept up by his global concerns until he began to speak about the specifics of the situation of the PKK in Turkey and in Europe. He fumbled around the details of Turkey's geography and seemed unsure of the acronyms of various groups associated with the PKK.

Is that all there is?

During the lunch break I went to an Internet café to doublecheck the background of the knowledgeable man. This initial search revealed that however authoritative his book on terrorism might be, there were very few copies in existence. It was cited in some footnotes but rarely quoted or otherwise mentioned in other books on the subject of terrorism. The search also indicated that his articles on terrorism related to the activities of animal rights groups.

That first morning I was shaken. I had worried that we would be dealing with a few malevolent types in this case, but I had always assumed that for the most part the people we were about to face would be intelligent and competent. Indeed, that assumption had been the basis of the lingering question in the back of my mind about Suleyman: *they must know something.*

That first morning, I realized that maybe they did not know much, if anything at all.

That afternoon I listened even more closely, and I detected what is called "padding" in academic essays. When you don't know what you are talking about, you try to dazzle others with the sheer volume of information. A paper blizzard can cover the reality that you do not know where you are going or exactly what you are trying to do. Over the coming months, throughout the hearings, that first impression would remain with me.

The two agents who had interviewed Suleyman in October 1994 were called upon to testify early in the complaint process. The woman was the first to appear, and it was the first time I learned her name. She seemed nervous and uncomfortable with being on the hot seat.

Barbara Jackman began to probe the agent's recollection of her interview with Suleyman. This was a crucial question because CSIS had claimed, at the outset of the review, that Suleyman had admitted he was a member of the PKK. I listened intently because I could not imagine how anyone could have come to that conclusion on the basis of what Suleyman had said during the interview.

The female agent struggled to remember details from the interview and said she had written her report on the interview two weeks after the meeting took place. She had used her notes as a basis for the report, but the notes were no longer available. Following general CSIS practice, she had discarded them after composing the report. Someone else, the agent said, someone higher up, had written the "final recommendation."

So it seemed that there was no direct evidence of what Suleyman said during the interview other than the notes I had taken and written up within hours of the interview and what the agent had later reported. It seemed as if what I remembered and what she remembered were quite different on some very important points. Barbara Jackman noted this and referred to the description of the interview as I had presented it in my book *At the Border Called Hope*. One of the most obvious points of disagreement regarded the actual length of the interview. I remembered that it lasted almost seven hours, and she now testified that it was only about five hours. Only? I also believed we had a very different recollection as to whether Suleyman had admitted in the interview that he was a member of the PKK.

At several points in the complaint process I found myself being forced to check and recheck my memory of certain events. At times

I had to say that I simply could not remember something or could not recall details clearly. But at other times I was much more certain about what was said during the interview of October 1994—and that was largely because of the notes I had taken, and because they had been written up within hours of the interrogation. I remembered clearly Suleyman's repeated denials that he was a member of the PKK, and I distinctly remembered that he had been propositioned by CSIS.[2]

The woman was questioned about her knowledge of the groups that Suleyman belonged to, and she was vague about the union that Suleyman had joined back in Turkey, and what kind of organization it was.

Still, the female agent at least seemed human. When her slight, bone-edged partner appeared in the boardroom he looked just as mean as ever—the kind of insecure, frightened man who is sometimes so dangerous. He repeated that Suleyman had admitted he was a member of the PKK. He was adamant on this point, sitting there with a slight smirk on his face. At one point Suleyman blew up: "You liar, you motherfucking liar!" Rae threatened to throw Suleyman out.

Once again Suleyman was in the grip of the dreaded *howl* of memory: the feeling of being absolutely powerless and at the mercy of an "uncle," the feeling of being, like his father, an innocent man falsely accused.

In his diary, written the night after the thin man testified, Suleyman served up a commentary. The man's French accent had set him off: "They want to affirm French language rights but don't recognize others. It's very nice to speak in your own language, but it seems the assimilation policy continues here too. Whenever we demand

Kurdish interpreters, they bring in Turkish interpreters, as if the two languages are the same."

The two CSIS agents were also interviewed in camera. When we received the summary report of those secret interviews, we were stunned. There was a clear indication that the CSIS claim about Suleyman admitting to being a member of the PKK *was not based on anything he said during the interview*. Instead, it was based on information from a "source." In other words, an informant told a CSIS agent that Suleyman had admitted to being a member of the PKK.

Another senior CSIS officer was called to testify regarding the use of "human sources" and whether immigration interviews should be used to recruit informants within ethnic communities. He expressed caution on the strategy of using "human sources," but was committed to it as a means of obtaining information about dangerous persons and groups. Still, he was adamantly against using the promise of immigrant papers as a way of eliciting information from refugees. He questioned the value of any information obtained in this way. This position had been expressed publicly by senior officials of CSIS and was repeated during this complaint process.

However, as we would soon learn, something quite different was happening on the ground. Throughout the SIRC hearing the pressure on Toronto's Kurdish community was intense. CSIS agents visited Kurds in their homes and asked questions about Suleyman. The Kurds were asked to sign papers saying Suleyman was a member of the PKK. This was blatant interference in the proceedings that were underway and in clear violation of directives that chairman Rae had given at the beginning of the proceedings. However, Suleyman insisted that most of the Kurds stood in solidarity with him; he was convinced that his struggle was their struggle.

Suleyman's lawyers followed a line of questioning that raised some of the more problematic aspects of using "human sources" or "informants."

As various agents testified, it became clear that their reliance on Kurdish informants had serious flaws—and in particular that the agents themselves knew little about the reality on which they were passing judgment. It became apparent that some members of the Kurdish community could exploit this situation. If Suleyman had his rivals for the leadership of the Kurdish community, CSIS had provided them with a perfect opportunity to rid themselves of a formidable opponent.

During the hearing, CSIS agents had visited various members of the Kurdish community and had met with H., the man who had forced Suleyman out of the Centre. H. had called a meeting to tell the community that CSIS was not intimidating members of the community. Suleyman became convinced that CSIS was controlling the Centre through proxies and that, in fact, the Service might itself be doing things to make the Centre look like a PKK front—as a way of criminalizing the Kurdish community. "I know guys who want to harm me, who want them to deport me," he told me. Suleyman also suspected that a smarmy Turkish interpreter who wanted to take away some of his business as a translator might also be acting as an informant. He thought, "The secret service has their feet within the community." He flailed away, struggling to find the names of his assailants.

Whoever they were, the informers had told CSIS that Suleyman admitted he was a member of the PKK. This false information convinced Suleyman that the main culprit could only be someone who held some kind of a serious grudge against him. "Nobody on earth, unless they are mentally retarded, would tell another person I am a member of this organization [the PKK]." For Suleyman, indeed, the most painful insight from the hearings was that he had been betrayed by members of his own community, for their own advantage. The tactics that CSIS used to inflict its own brand of terror on the community had been deftly manipulated by people within the community for their own purposes. Experts on Kurdistan have called this the double oppression of the people—by the Turkish masters but also by their own leaders, who savaged each other as much as they were persecuted by the Turks. The Kurdish people had always been let down by the rivalries and treacheries of the Kurdish leaders, and this internal destruction had been a major reason why they had not been able to achieve even some form of cultural independence.

Suleyman knew about this long history of betrayal. It had cost his father his life, and it was now denying the son not just his peace but his place in his chosen country.

Towards the end of the hearing it seemed as if the "source" who had fingered Suleyman had been identified and completely discredited. We could only infer this finding from the summaries of the secret hearings and from remarks made by the SIRC lawyers. In any case, the final report contained pointed remarks about the reliance on human sources who may have their own agendas.

Throughout the long hearing Barbara Jackman and Sharry Aiken continued to probe a central issue raised by the complaint. What is a terrorist group? Who defines a terrorist group? What does it mean to be a member of a terrorist group? They posed these questions again and again to the various CSIS officers who testified.

The law does not offer a specific definition; and the many and various descriptions given by CSIS officers in the hearing indicated that their definition of "terrorist group" was by no means exact.

Was it a group that acted violently against innocent civilians? Well, then, perhaps the bombing of Baghdad, in which many innocent civilians were killed, could be construed as a terrorist act. Or was this an act of war? And who decides? The exchanges we had on this issue were important and insightful, but it became clear to us that the csis officers preferred a nebulous state of affairs regarding definition because it gave them more latitude for action.

As for the question of what constitutes membership in a terrorist group, does it mean having a membership card? Does it mean reading newspapers? Does it mean sympathizing with the goals of a group (for example, the pkk) but not necessarily their means? Does it mean contributing money to pay the rent of a community-based centre? Does it mean committing violent acts?

Again, the csis agents clearly preferred not to define what constituted "membership." They seemed to be saying simply that you would know one when you see one. For the various csis agents, "membership in a terrorist group" was more a state of being than something defined by specific actions. This lack of definition places an enormous responsibility on individual officers and gives incredible discretionary power to the intelligence service. (See the discussion of these issues in Appendix A.)

As I listened to the various discussions—and learned a great deal in the process—I realized that csis would not welcome any effort to place restrictions on its almost unrestricted ability to file someone away into the category of being a "member of a terrorist group."

• • •

As the hearing ground on, certain rituals developed. At noon hour, with the exception of Bob Rae, we would all go down to a coffee shop on the main floor of the Eaton Centre. Suleyman and his lawyers and I would sit a few tables away from the Justice Department lawyers. We would exchange a few pleasantries. One of the government lawyers, I discovered, knew a friend of mine from Timmins. I came to feel that the lawyers for CSIS were just doing their job as competently as they could, that they had no personal axe to grind, that they were life-sized. Suleyman was not so sure. "She's a pretty woman, but she looks devilish," he said of one of the lawyers. He told me how once they were having a chat—it was on a Friday after the session was over—and she said she was going home to Ottawa because she had a dog at home alone. Suleyman remarked that it might be difficult for the dog to be alone, "because animals are very sensitive." When she asked him if he liked animals, he suspected it was because she believed that terrorists should not like animals.

Towards the end of the hearing a single piece of paper surfaced, and I still do not know where to file it. After we became aware of the contradiction between my memory of the length of the October interview (seven hours) and the officers' (less than five hours), we had tried to find the original call-in notice, which would indicate a time for the interview. Suleyman had kept the original notice in his briefcase, together with newspaper articles about the death of his father and other matters. However, his briefcase had been stolen shortly before the SIRC hearing. He had given a copy of the notice to a lawyer, who would not take the time to find Suleyman's file. So Suleyman went to the Immigration office in Etobicoke to ask for a copy. He waited there for several hours until the person at the desk finally told him that there was no notice in his file, or perhaps it had been removed.

To rebut my testimony, the lawyers for CSIS tabled a copy of the call-in notice, which indicated that the interview was scheduled for

10:00 a.m. and not 9:00 a.m., as I recalled. The notice was passed across the table to me, and as Sharry Aiken questioned its origins I kept looking at it; and as I read the details on the piece of paper and saw the time recorded on it I began to feel completely disoriented. I felt that my grip on reality was fragile at best. I knew what I remembered, but then again maybe I did not.

I kept looking. I knew something was wrong, either with me or with the document. Then I realized that the notice, addressed to Suleyman Goven, presented his current address, on Appleton Avenue—and not Quebec Avenue, where he had lived in 1994. Clearly the document had been retrofitted.

I passed a note over to Sharry signalling the difference, punctuated with something like "!!!????" She immediately drew the discrepancy in the document to the attention of the chair. It was one of the few moments in the hearings when Bob Rae became noticeably upset. "Technically, the document is a forgery," he said. He went on:

> If I wanted to be technical, I would say that this is a forged document, because it is a document that purports to be something which it is not.
>
> The computer does not act on its own. The computer does not spit out these documents in its spare time. The computer responds to human instructions. Somebody instructed the computer to come up with this document, and it is a forgery.
>
> I take a very dim view of the Department of Immigration handing in documents that are falsified. . . . I think it is appalling.
>
> I am not blaming you personally for it. I think it is a crummy practice.

It makes you wonder about other documents; that's all. If they have the technological capability of doing a bunch of things, you worry about what else is possible to do in terms of the dating of evidence and everything else.

It is not smart.[3]

The lawyer for csis was also clearly upset. He pointed out that the document had been given to his legal team by the Immigration Department, that it was not from the legal team, and said he would check into the situation immediately. It was as if all the oxygen went out of the air.

That was a time when the old harpy of fear whispered: They can change documents and evidence to fit whatever reality they want. They can do whatever they want.

And why? Why was it so important to prove they were right on such a minor point?

• • •

I had now seen the csis agents up close and personal. I saw their faces and now knew their names, and so had Suleyman. The faceless, nameless ones had become real people. It was obvious that they were not demons. They were ordinary people, and they had done a lot of damage. And the Canadian public will never know their names or see their faces.

It was evident that Canadian lawmakers had placed enormous power in the hands of very ordinary people who made mistakes, as most ordinary people do. Yet it also became clear that these ordinary people who worked in csis were reluctant to admit that they ever did make mistakes. Perhaps if they had been better trained they might have felt more secure in sifting and sorting information, and in making appropriate, informed adjustments, but apparently they had not been effectively prepared for this complicated task.

Over the months of the hearing these agents had hummed and hawed and invoked a vague sense of national security every time they were unsure of themselves. The agents had been placed in a situation of evaluating data from a community and a country without having the necessary language skills and without knowing the history and politics of the country. Most of the information they supplied was second-hand, from sources such as the Turkish intelligence agency, the CIA (a close ally of Turkey), and local informants.

The hearings concluded. The chairman noted that it was the lengthiest and most thorough review in the history of the Security Intelligence Review Committee. Indeed, it had come at great expense to the Canadian taxpayer. For each session four lawyers would fly in from Ottawa and stay at hotels; a recording clerk would fly in for the technical services; two lawyers were being paid by legal aid to represent Suleyman; a chairman was being paid to oversee the process. Then there was the time and money associated with calling the various witnesses for CSIS and Suleyman. It had been a serious undertaking.

We waited over a year for the results of the hearing. During that time, though, I felt that the entire procedure had in some way been a healing process for Suleyman. Despite its rather bizarre aspects, the hearing had a sense of fairness, of issues fairly contested. It seemed that due process had been followed.

Although it was still night, Suleyman no longer felt quite so alone. Although he had been undoubtedly betrayed by some members of his community, others there had remained faithful to him.

He wrote in his diary: "During those sessions we tried to discover our friends and enemies. And I didn't receive any help or assistance from the Centre, where I was accused. I had to testify because of their wrongdoings. I know because of those irresponsible and poor individuals . . . we had a rough time."

Finally, in April 2000, almost three years after the complaint was first filed, the final report on Suleyman's complaint arrived. The report was sent to Sharry Aiken, who immediately phoned everyone concerned. The report presented a strong and forceful recommendation that Suleyman be granted his landed papers. The phone lines hummed with satisfaction and relief. Suleyman had won!

We read the lengthy report carefully. In his adjudication Bob Rae noted that the concept of "membership" in terrorism had been used so loosely that it "casts a very wide net, and that a great many people who are politically active Kurdish nationalists, who are peaceful, law abiding and non-violent, will be labeled as 'terrorists.' In my view, that is exactly what has happened in the case of Mr. Goven. He has been unfairly labeled. He is not a member of a terrorist organization."

The report referred to one of the probable sources of this label. "Nor is a simple assertion by a human source that someone else is a member of the PKK a 'fact.' It is an expression of opinion from within a beleaguered community where rumour and gossip inevitably feed on each other. Someone could well have a personal grudge, and how damaging such an opinion could be when given to CSIS (usually for money). It is difficult to see how much stock can be placed on this kind of information."

The report made several other recommendations relating to policy and procedures. Perhaps one of the most important was that all security interviews be taped so that if a dispute occurs over exactly what was said by either the refugee or the officer, reference can be made to the tapes. It also recommended that the Service be held accountable for delays due to its own processes and that if the delay were to be longer than twelve months, "the individual concerned be informed in writing of a right to initiate a complaint with the review committee."

The report concluded with a specific recommendation: "that the Service inform CIC [Immigration Canada], that the Security Intelligence Review Committee has recommended that the Complainant's application be processed for landing."

It was a triumphant moment for Suleyman. A press conference at Queen's Park announced the results of his complaint and his complete vindication. He conducted several press interviews. In May, based on his commitment to justice, not only for himself but also for all refugees, Suleyman was named refugee of the year by the Canadian Council for Refugees. A ceremony was held at Metro City Hall to present the award. "In my high school years I received medals as an athlete and cross-country runner, but since that time I never got any awards," Suleyman said. "I consider this award as a political one because I have been fighting for refugees for eight years." For Suleyman, it was a great honour that a Canadian organization was recognizing—and offering praise for—his work.

CSIS had been "studying" the SIRC report long before its public release, and almost immediately the agency issued a statement challenging the findings. According to one report, Dan Lambert, a CSIS spokesman, maintained that "the central issue raised by SIRC is the definition of who is a member of a terrorist group." Lambert noted that "CSIS has taken a broad interpretation of the term 'membership' based on a series of court rulings." CSIS was clearly unwilling to let go of its power to define just who was a terrorist: "The courts have ruled that the term 'membership' should be given an 'unrestricted and broad' interpretation when national security is at stake." According to Lambert, speaking for csis, "Our view is that the courts have done a good job of defining the issue."4

Two months later another news story told of a "lengthy rebuttal" in which csis defended its position against the sirc report. Documents that the newspaper obtained through an Access to Information request indicated that csis was "disturbed" by the report, and especially by the watchdog committee's suggestion that the intelligence service needed to adopt a more limited definition of "membership" in a terrorist group. According to the article, one document noted, "The committee gives insufficient consideration to the impact of ignoring terrorist support activity in Canada on our national interests and our good standing in the international community." In other words, csis is right and those who criticize it are wrong. The documents gave warning of the dire consequences that would come from following the sirc recommendations: "Canada will be viewed as an 'active sponsor' of terrorism if it allows supporters of violent extremist groups to operate on its soil."5

On Suleyman's behalf Andrew Brouwer did his own Access to Information request for documents written by csis on the subject of Suleyman Goven. It took almost three and a half years to obtain a sheaf of documents that were mostly blacked out. One particularly shocking document indicates that csis was determined very early on to ignore the report from the Honourable Robert Rae. In a statement dated February 17, 2000—two months before the sirc report was made public—csis wrote its "secret" comments. It questioned whether sirc had any jurisdiction to make specific recommendations regarding Suleyman Goven. It swept aside at least two major conclusions of the report: "The Service continues to stand by its assessment that there are reasonable grounds to believe Mr. Goven was, at the time of his immigration security screening interview, a member of the PKK." Regarding the complaint that CSIS used the immigration screening interview to recruit informants, the document said, "Mr. Goven's complaint, and the suggestion which was made to the press in April 1998 and to a Parliamentary Committee, that CSIS recruits paid informers through the immigration security screening process is manifestly unfounded."[6]

• • •

The struggle with the faceless one, the nameless one, was not over. It would take us some time to realize how ineffective the whole complaint process had been. We were naive enough to think that Suleyman would receive his landed immigrant papers at his earliest convenience. There was no phone call; no letter; no sign that the SIRC report had landed on anyone's desk anywhere. Once again the ambiguous nature of the relationship between CSIS and Canada Immigration served the nameless ones well. According to CSIS officers, their job is simply to make recommendations to Immigration, but they do not make the final decision. The final decision is made by the Department of Citizenship and Immigration, and ultimately by the Minister of Citizenship, Immigration, and Multiculturalism. However, according to Canada Immigration officers, they would never go against the recommendations of CSIS. Ministers of Immigration have said something to the same effect: "No Immigration Minister would dare to go against CSIS."[7]

Within Canada Immigration a unit called Immigration Security has a role that is less than clear. It may have a stated purpose of bridging between CSIS and Immigration, but what it instead provides is a yawning gap. It is a gap that was identified during Suleyman's complaint process. As I described it in my testimony (which the Rae report quoted):

> In the present situation, the division of responsibilities results in a Pilate-like situation of irresponsibility in which everyone can wash his or her own hands. csis officers can claim that they only give advice to Immigration Security. However, when you talk with Immigration Security officers they say they are only following the advice of csis. No one has to face the refugee whose life lands in the balance. . . . No one is responsible for mistakes and no one has to face the consequences of their decisions.

When the summer of 2000 arrived and Suleyman had still not yet received his permanent residence papers, Andrew Brouwer began phoning the Immigration Department to ask about the delay. He found out that csis had sent the Department some "new" information that put in question sirc's recommendation for Suleyman to be landed. I phoned the office of the Minister of Immigration repeatedly and explained the situation to her senior staff. How can the Minister ignore the recommendations of the Security Intelligence Review Committee? The members of the staff seemed to be reluctant to get involved. They were unsure of how to deal with the amount of information they were receiving, not only from us but from others as well. To this day I am not certain that they read Rae's report or, if they did, whether they understood its implications.

After many more months of lobbying, Suleyman was finally granted another interview with Immigration. It was almost a year after sirc issued its recommendation. Once again the members of the Sanctuary group accompanied Suleyman to the Immigration office in Etobicoke. He was to be represented by Andrew, who by that time was becoming something of an expert in security law. We thought this would be a simple matter. After all, SIRC had made a crystal-clear recommendation.

It was not to be. The person in charge, a middle-aged woman named Anne Dello, was the Immigration officer who had twice interviewed Suleyman.[8] Andrew began by asking her if she had read the SIRC report, with its clear recommendation that Suleyman be landed. She said she had not read the report and was under no obligation to read it. She repeated the by-now familiar accusations: that he might be a member of the PKK, that the Centre was a front for the PKK. This time, though, there was a new twist: in 1997 the Centre had supposedly been engaged in raising money for a missile!

The arrogance of this woman was appalling, but we had no way of knowing if she had anything to do with the decision to ignore the SIRC report. After such an intensive and costly process, *someone* had decided that the report was irrelevant. I made repeated calls to Elinor Caplan, the minister of immigration, and to her "senior staff," trying to get some movement. I wrote and wrote. It just did not make sense: SIRC had delivered such a strong recommendation; and people in the Immigration Department had not even read the report.

Even the Minister of Immigration seemed incapable of resolving the situation. She had to rely on her senior staff, and her senior staff was juggling so many things that it could scarcely immerse itself in the intricacies of immigration security, Kurds in Turkey, and what have you. The staff was going to be easily impressed by officers who claimed to have written authoritative books on terrorism and who had large wads of paper about the situation in Turkey and who had made such accurate notes during the interview with Suleyman Goven.

As far as I know, none of Rae's recommendations were ever implemented. Sylvia MacKenzie, the lead lawyer for SIRC, resigned after finding out that the Review Board's recommendations would be completely disregarded by Immigration Canada and CSIS. When I heard this news I phoned her to say I was sorry that she was leaving her position. She was despondent—saying that she believed she had given some assurance to us that justice would be done . . . and it wasn't. She began to cry and then hung up.

The injustice was so glaring that I knew a great deal of political will would be required to fix it. Repairing the situation seemed to require two cabinet ministers, the Solicitor General (who was in charge of CSIS), and the Immigration Minister. As far as I could see, there were civil servants who liked things just the way they were.

I called Chaviva Hošek, a former senior policy analyst to Prime Minister Jean Chrétien, to get her suggestions on how to proceed. She suggested I call Eddie Goldenberg, who was in charge of guiding the Liberal ship of state as the Prime Minister's senior political advisor. On April 2, 2001 (a year after the SIRC recommendation had been issued), I took the train to Ottawa to meet with Goldenberg in the Langevin Block.

Goldenberg has been called "cherubic," but no one would call him innocent. We chatted amiably about some mutual friends, and then I told him I wanted to describe the black hole into which people were disappearing. I told him about the endless October interview I had witnessed, and about the Kurdish refugees from Turkey. Goldenberg's response was: "CSIS is racist and incompetent and does not want interference from anyone. Imagine how they would react if the PMO got involved."

He wondered why CSIS was "even interested" in this situation. "Maybe the CIA would be interested because of their relationship with Turkey, but it's not important for us." Goldenberg said he would do something and I promised to get him the names of people who could give some specific suggestions about how to plug the black hole in the system.

On the train back to Toronto, thoughts chugged through my mind. *Does he really think Canada has no interest in Turkey?*

He doesn't care.

He doesn't care.

He doesn't care.

Soon after our conversation, Goldenberg himself was in the middle of a huge political struggle as the Liberal Party tried to decide between Martin and Chrétien as leader.

Suleyman received a letter from Immigration saying that he would not be receiving landed immigrant status because of "security concerns," but that he could continue to stay in the country to work and/or study. The attempt to stigmatize Suleyman continued and was starting to have an impact on the Kurds he was trying to help. Just after New Year's Day in 2003 a Kurdish family entered Canada through the Fort Erie port of entry. One of their relatives asked Suleyman to go to the border to translate for the family. The Immigration officer who interviewed them attached this memo to their file. "PC [Suleyman] is suspected to be affiliated with Kurdish Terrorist Group. Arrived at POE [port of entry] after family. Said he was paged to do so. Suspected Agent, noted on refugee claimants file that Minister's Intervention requested for any further clients that Suleyman Goven meets."[9]

The reference to "Minister's Intervention" means that this refugee family, and anyone else that Suleyman would translate for, would be questioned by a representative from the Minister of Immigration's Office to raise questions specifically related to security. The burden of the refugee hearing would now weigh doubly on the refugee family.

Suleyman and Barbara Jackman decided to turn to the courts to ask for a judicial review of the Immigration Department's decision not to consider the report from SIRC. Between the time that the application for judicial review was filed and the hearing, another year passed.

On April 5, 2001, at the Federal Court of Canada on University Avenue in Toronto, Barbara argued that the Immigration Department had to take account of the SIRC recommendation that Suleyman get his landed immigrant papers. The lawyer for the Immigration Department argued that they were not obliged to read the report.

Some nineteen months later, on November 12, 2002, the Federal Court judge ruled that the Minister of Citizenship and Immigration (and the officials of the department) must read the report of the Intelligence Review Committee before making a decision about Suleyman Goven's status:

> In her decision, the officer makes no mention of the SIRC report. She simply makes the blanket statement that she considered "the information you provided and that contained [sic] on file." The officer was the final decision maker and she was not bound by the SIRC report. However, given that the report was the result of a lengthy, complex, and official hearing which directly addressed the issue of the applicant's possible membership in the PKK, and reached a conclusion opposite to that of the officer, she should have explained her rejection of it.
>
> The respondent argues that the SIRC report is irrelevant because it considers whether the applicant was a member of the PKK, rather than investigating the link between the TKCIC

[Kurdish Information Centre] and the PKK, which was the basis for the officer's decision. The SIRC report would, in fact, be far more relevant to this case than the evidence linking the TKCIC to the PKK, since it more directly addresses the central issue.[10]

The judge ordered that another Immigration officer review Suleyman's application for landed immigrant status.

Still, nothing happened. No one responded to the judicial order. Suleyman's lawyer contacted someone in Immigration, who acknowledged that the department should read the SIRC report—although, this person added, the department was under no obligation to do so quickly. By that point the constant refusal to grant Suleyman his papers seemed not just callous and careless but stubborn and stupid. Was it a simple reluctance to admit that anyone had done anything wrong?

Yet was it also something more, something more than personal?

The security legislation, which gives immense powers to individual security officers, rests entirely on the assumption that a definition of terrorism or of what membership in a terrorist group means is not necessary because the officers who make this judgment are qualified. It rests on the assumption that they can use this enormous power in a judicious way because they never make mistakes.

Enormous power rests in the hands of people who are not accountable. If the struggle of Suleyman reveals anything, it is that neither CSIS nor Immigration intelligence is under any public control. CSIS has not implemented any of the recommendations of the SIRC report, and the Immigration intelligence system does not have any outside watchdog.

When the twin towers exploded in New York in 2001, the pressure on all suspected terrorists was increased. A new Security Bill gave even more power and required even less accountability from security agents and those conducting interviews. In 2002 CSIS placed the PKK on the official terrorist list. The listing was a little out of date given that the leader of the PKK had been captured in 1999 and that ever since 1998 the group had renounced violent military actions and had been pushing for a negotiated political settlement to the Kurdish question. By 2002 the PKK had not been advocating so much separatism as some expanded form of cultural autonomy.[11]

The tragedy of 9/11 brought an immediate influx of cash to the security services and led to the creation of the new Canada Border Security Agency. Hundreds of new recruits scurried into the arms of CSIS. Several reports indicate that the sudden increase in numbers has not brought an increase in competence. In the Auditor General's report of March 2004, Sheila Fraser noted a complete disarray in the "watch lists" used to screen refugee claimants and others seeking to enter Canada.[12]

As for Suleyman, he could only worry about others who were falsely accused. He saw a young Kurdish boy picked up for shoplifting. The boy had not understood the English questions being put to him. "My dear brother, this is your first surprise," Suleyman wrote in his diary. "And I don't know how many you will face throughout your life. You are not the first victim."

Suleyman had sought recourse through trusted procedures in this country—the Security Intelligence Review Committee and the Federal Court. And still the struggle with *someone* was not over. He had been wounded in the process; something of his enthusiasm about Canada had been crushed. "I have not found peace here."

THE BREAK OF DAY

I T WAS not yet daybreak.

Wave after wave of darkness was pulling the light back into its undertow.

Although the night had not yet broken, Suleyman was almost broken. I was almost broken. We limped, and somehow the faceless, nameless opponent lumbered on. Clumsily, crazily.

The curtain of the night could not be lifted by truth, not by rule of law, not by sheer persistence.

In that long night I began to realize that something was broken in this country. A great wound, an original sin, was keeping us from our original blessing.

Something of my feeling for my country had crumpled within. I found it hard to sing the national anthem. I was reluctant to wear my Order of Canada pin. I knew that Suleyman had not given up. Yet I also knew that the struggle was on the verge of destroying him. I had not given up; I just felt as though I had nothing more to give.

• • •

And yet. And yet. Sometimes things give way. Sometimes when hope seems to disappear it reappears around some unexpected corner.

For Suleyman, it came on a bus ride to London, Ontario, and in the form of a woman. Although he always wrote in his diary in times of immense stress and sorrow, at the time of this encounter, in October 1999, he wrote out of extreme vulnerability.

I wonder if I am in love? I was travelling to London and the first bus was full so I had to take the second one, which was half empty. There were a lot of vacant seats and I saw a lady sitting by herself. She was writing something. Sometimes she closed her eyes and seemed to have deep thoughts and then she kept on writing. Then she looked at me and I smiled at her. I didn't have anything to do. I didn't even have a newspaper. I just kept watching her. Two people in front of me kept talking. One of them was really cheerful. When we passed the Hilton Hotel, he said that was where he worked. Since he was so noisy I could hear what they were talking about. Towards the middle of the journey, the lady asked this guy if she could borrow his newspaper. Then she gave it to me. Then she asked if she could sit with me.

Without hesitation I said yes. I didn't want to read the newspaper. I just wanted to talk with her. She said she was preparing a speech for a prayer service at her church in Sarnia. She was a pleasant person, about thirty years old, and she told me she was married to a man who was fifty-two years old, but they were not together anymore.

During the journey she shared her water and her food with me. She told me that when she had closed her eyes before, she was trying to figure out if I was a good person or a bad person.

She said it's a kind of psychic thing with her. Eventually she had decided that I was a good person and she could talk with me. The time passed quickly.

Usually I sleep on a trip but this time I didn't. When we arrived in London her mother was waiting for her. She told me she had to take another bus to Sarnia. Her mother hugged me also. When we said goodbye to each other she kissed me on my cheek.

I called Kathleen and then again last Friday I took the 2:30 bus to London [en route to Sarnia]. I called her but I didn't say I was going to visit. Before we got to London the driver said the bus for Sarnia would leave from platform 6. I got confused about whether I should go to Sarnia but then I decided to go. Before the bus left, I called her but no one was home. After I arrived in Sarnia, I called and they were at home. She came with her mother's car to pick me up. She made a lentil meal. She told me she was a good cook. After that she drove me around Sarnia. She showed me where she grew up, where she went to school, a lot of things. She told me her parents had divorced when she was small. She showed me the house they owned before it got sold. After this tour with the car, we went for a walk. She held my hand, [and we were] like two lovers. We walked a lot. I wanted to hold her, but I didn't have the courage. We walked around for about an hour. Later she made a bed for me, but I didn't feel I wanted to go to bed. I told her I would watch TV. Before she said goodnight, she hugged me.

In the morning she knocked at the door. She was dressed already. She came in and sat down on the bed and I just touched her face and just looked at her. It was a very nice feeling. After a small breakfast she took me to the bus station, and on the way again we held hands. I said, "I love you," and she repeated the same thing. It was a beautiful feeling. Before I got on the bus we hugged each other and kissed each other on the cheeks. I haven't forgotten her since I returned. I feel like she is in my mind all the time.

I talked to her again today. I wanted to meet her at the bus station in Toronto, but she wanted to walk to my place. I wanted to spend more time with her.

The relationship continued off and on for about two years, even to the point that Suleyman would bring her to some of the Romero House social events. In the end the differences between these two people, although healing, would prove to be too great. She was into a new-age lifestyle and personal healing, and Suleyman was much more politically oriented.

Yet she had awakened something, a vulnerability, in Suleyman and revealed to him that he still had the capacity to trust, to love.

Once I got a sense of this relationship, I started to tease him about getting married. Teasing was my most effective way of making a point with Suleyman because I had learned, long ago, that he had become immune to lectures or admonitions.

"Suleyman, you should get married. Think of it! This would drive the uncles crazy to see you laughing and dancing and getting on with your life. It would drive them nuts to see you populating the world with little Suleymans and Suleyettes. They would come to your wedding and take pictures of everything, and they would go back and look at them and be totally jealous. It would drive them crazy!"

He would howl, this time with laughter in his voice. Giggle even. He would place his hand over his mouth, barely containing his delight, like a small boy. In the laughter something gave way. From my Irish relatives I have learned that oppressed people often use humour as their first form of freedom. It becomes a way of refusing to let the oppressor define the nature of reality.

It was around this time that I began to call Suleyman "our friendly local terrorist." I would introduce him that way to people and quickly add, "Every community needs one." People would gawk, he would giggle, and we would all crack up.

The joke dispelled some kind of demons in us all. We embraced the burden of his label and said it didn't matter. He was not a label; he was a person with a label. He was friendly and local.

• • •

The night was unbroken, but Suleyman was not alone. There were others with him, struggling towards daybreak, limping now but still leaning towards the light.

By 2004 Andrew Brouwer had finished his law studies and was ready to immerse himself in Suleyman's case. Andrew was determined, fresh with energy and moral intelligence. He had been mulling over Suleyman's situation with the Sanctuary Coalition. We had seen the Immigration officers brush off the results of the SIRC recommendation and the ruling of the Federal Court. After many meetings we inched towards thinking that perhaps a civil suit for damages would break the hold of the security and immigration systems.

Perhaps, we thought, if money was involved the system would have to clean up its act. If there was a potential for a lawsuit every time a security interview and decision took more than a year, the pressure might lead to systemic change. If there was a potential for a lawsuit every time an officer was not able to bear the burden of proof, then there would be change. If large sums of money were involved each and every time refugees sued for the great damage done to their lives, there would be change, and fast. If the lawsuits named names and times and places and called individuals to account, there would be change. If those who acted and decided could not hide behind the blindfold of the system, there would be change.

We resolved that taking legal action would be a way of moving towards a form of public accountability that the political system seemed unwilling or unable to provide.

Andrew and his friend Hadayt Nazami had now teamed up with Barbara Jackman in a law firm, and they decided that the best route to pursue was a class action suit for damages, naming both csis and the Immigration Department. They put out a call through various refugee networks asking if there were people whose lives had been severely damaged because of the security screening process. To our surprise and distress, fifty people came forward: fifty people who had fallen into the black hole of the security system; fifty people whose lives had been put on hold for years.

Andrew and his team began to assemble the data slowly, methodically. They wanted to ensure that each claim was solid. However, Andrew and the rest of us were also aware that the minute this kind of case moved towards the courts, the Immigration Department and/or csis would instruct its lawyers to resolve the matter out of court rather than have a case set a precedent for others.

We all wanted such a settlement for the individuals, but we also knew that only systemic change, a precedent set, would bring about effective justice for all of the refugees who were struggling with a hidden system that had the potential to wound them grievously. Given the amount of work involved, Andrew had to be sure that at least one person would not settle, that at least one person would see the process of justice through to the end.

He knew that person was Suleyman Goven, and Suleyman knew that he was meant to be that person. And so the case was called *Suleyman Goven v. The Attorney General of Canada.*

The suit was filed in Federal Court on November 9, 2005. It will be years in the legal system before the dawn breaks and the system will break down; and it will take millions of dollars to repair the damage, to mend the crack in the system.[1]

For Suleyman, this new legal action led to a new sense of calling. It was as if he had accepted the price of leadership, once again. He recognized that it would continue to be a long struggle, and that anyone who took up a leadership role in a tightly knit community was asking for trouble. "When many people love you there are usually enemies," he said. "You should expect this. Sometimes people will hurt you even if you try to help them. This is the fate of community leaders."

He did have enemies, but he also had a new and very elderly friend. My mother, Rita Leddy, attended the sessions at the Federal Court over the next two years. She had come to admire his tenacity. "You haven't given up Suleyman, and you haven't given in," she told him. "What you are doing is right and important." Whenever she came into the courtroom he would rise and greet her, shake her hand, and bow.

• • •

At the same time hope stood up and was counted in the House of Commons. On the evening of April 21, 2004, the House of Commons passed a motion condemning the brutal treatment of the

Armenians in Turkey, calling it an act of genocide. Some five years prior to this, when a similar motion was introduced, it had been finessed by the government in a way that would not offend the Turkish government while giving a nod to the Armenian reality. In 1998 a motion was passed that referred to the 1915 events as a "calamity" and a "tragic event."

In 2004, once again there had been enormous pressure from the Turkish government to tone down the motion or to abandon it altogether. Foreign Affairs Minister Bill Graham and a high-powered business lobby had warned the parliamentarians that there could be serious repercussions for Canadian trade with Turkey, especially for the Canadian businesses that had more than $1 billion in potential contracts there. In the charged caucus meeting in the morning, Graham warned the MPs that companies such as Bombardier Aerospace and SNC-Lavalin could lose out to European companies for megaprojects such as the extension of the Ankara subway system.

The Canadian Chamber of Commerce had written a letter to all of the members of Parliament, warning, "There will be an immediate negative economic impact on Canadian firms and their ability to do business in Turkey."[2]

It was not an idle threat. In 2001 the French government had adopted a similar resolution on the Armenian genocide, and Turkey had cancelled multimillion-dollar defence contracts with that country.

Despite this pressure, seventy-eight Liberal backbenchers broke ranks with the cabinet, as did some members of the Conservative Party. The NDP and Bloc Québécois voted for the motion. Despite the dire warnings of the business community, the Prime Minister had allowed a free vote, although he himself was not present for it.

MP Stan Dromisky, not surprisingly, voted against the motion.

In moving the motion, MP Madeleine Dalphond-Guiral (Laval Centre, BQ) urged her fellow members to support the motion "to ensure that historical justice is rendered and give ourselves the tools we need to build a better world." She continued: "During their lives, individuals and peoples are often wounded. The deeper the wounds, the longer it takes to heal. I truly believe that by acknowledging the genocide perpetrated on the Armenian people, we will be helping to heal their scars."[3]

The motion marked an ethical moment in the Canadian Parliament and one that, in retrospect, will stand in the history books as a time when considerations of trade were not allowed to override a human rights issue. All of the CANDU reactors, all of the light-rail transit deals, all of the pipelines and the U.S. strategic and economic interests did not dissuade the regular members of Parliament from acknowledging the tragic suffering of other human beings.

The Government of Canada that had said "no" to the war in Iraq was now saying "no" to the pressure from Turkey. It meant that the night might be long, but it would not be endless.

•　•　•

Hope also danced in the sky at night, in the form of the northern lights. Suleyman had not found a secure place in Canadian society, but for three summers he made the trek north with the Romero House community to attend our annual summer camp. There he found a different kind of home in this land.

In the summer, for us, the direction of hope lies north. Every summer since 1992 Romero House has taken refugees from the city north to our camp held at the Anishinabe Spiritual Centre near Espanola, Ontario. We go north to a place where the fish swim deep, the sky blooms and billows, and the birds fly high above any checkpoint. It is where the province's rugged landscape begins. It is the beginning not of mountains but of rocks, of jagged scars, of rivers and waterfalls. It is the home place of fish and wolves and the first peoples. In the summers of 1997, 1998, and 1999 we invited Suleyman to go along because we knew he needed to get away. Little did we know he was going home.

When Suleyman arrived at the camp he quickly went through an unexpected transformation. This slow and stooped man began to stand up straight. As he ran around in evening soccer games he seemed to forget about his limp. He was still an aggressive player, and a good one, and he lost himself in the game. He seemed younger.

He was completely taken with the story of the aboriginal peoples of the area and would talk with them for hours when they would come by the Centre. He was interested in their history and their spirituality. I realized that he was also an aboriginal, one of the first peoples who belonged to the land more than the land belonged to them. He realized that too.

Kurds are one of the indigenous peoples. There is a reserve about half an hour from the Anishinabe Centre. I was told that they have two schools in their mother language and that the band has companies dealing with lumber and construction. If this kind of opportunity was offered to my people, we could live in a free atmosphere with the Turks as brothers. It would be nice. This is good for indigenous people because they are the real owners of this land.

One of the Kurds joked that perhaps they should apply for aboriginal status in Canada and then they would not have to pay taxes. On July 24, 1999, Suleyman wrote:

> Today is my third visit to Anishinabe Spiritual Centre. After arriving here, mother nature welcomed us again with a heavy rain. This place was built twenty years ago. It was built under the influence of the Indian people. At the entrance there are bird feathers in different colours which indicate the four different directions. There are pictures all over the buildings about the aboriginal people. The building is constructed with wood. There is a tree of life which symbolizes the beliefs of the aboriginal people. There is also a circle which symbolizes the four seasons and four directions. When I look at this life tree I realize that human beings are in harmony with other creatures. The place where I was born is a good example of this. Nobody hunts wild animals there anymore and the four seasons are those of a human being's life. You are born at point zero and you die at point zero. In the humid and hot weather of July mother nature offers us a nice atmosphere. This place overlooks Anderson Lake and it is a wonderful place.

Suleyman attended the Christian liturgies presided over by Father Jack Costello, the Jesuit who was the chaplain of the Romero House community. Father Costello explained the various aboriginal symbols that could be seen in the large log chapel looking out over the lake. Suleyman noted: "He talked about the picture of the life tree. He said that the juices represent both male and female in the life tree. At the bottom of the life tree are monsters showing their feet and that represent the danger a plant has to face."

But Suleyman was not totally sure about these Christians. He wondered about what would happen if these Catholic people— "who say Peace to each other"—were suddenly to be set down in Turkey. "I don't know what would happen to them." He was also not totally romantic about the struggle of the aboriginal peoples.

> This is an aboriginal nation on the verge of annihilation because of massacres and diseases. And they are the real owners of Canada. But now the French and English are the owners and they are judging the refugee claims as if the aboriginal peoples are guests in their own land. . . . If you destroy mother nature then you destroy your own future.

Suleyman had talked with someone from the Fox tribe.

> I read a book that said the King of France decided to annihilate the Fox tribe. According to this plan, if someone resisted then he or she would be killed and would be taken as a slave and sold in the market in France. This was a vicious plan of annihilation. But the Fox tribe resisted and France had to make truce with them. Because the aboriginals understood that if they co-operated with the French it would mean their end. In the Kurdish cause there was always a big betrayal. But the hope of the Kurdish people never diminished.

He was amazed, too, by the harmony of the northern land. He wrote in his diary about how he spent time simply walking around, studying "mother nature" and thinking about her:

I know that when people die of the most terrible diseases and
are murdered, our mother opens her arms and welcomes them
all, like a very passionate mother. I felt like I heard a cry from
the deepness of history in the wind where the ancestors of the
aboriginal people cry, a cry of thousands of years.

One day I was working in the kitchen when Valerie Walsh, the
camp director, came in and said, "You should go to the chapel and
see who is sitting there." I went to the door of the little chapel that
was underneath the larger one. It was surrounded by windows that
opened out onto the lake and then onto the trees and rocks. There in
the rocking chair by the window was Suleyman, asleep and at peace.

I could hardly look at him—he was so quiet, in such original
innocence. *You were meant for this,* I thought. As he himself put it:

If I say the most peaceful moment of my life was during the
one-week camp at Anishinabe, it wouldn't be an exaggeration.
If we say that peace is in every step and if we carry out this principle, we will be happy and safe from stress. Anishinabe is my
peace place in Canada. During one week, no sounds of a car,
no appointments, no rush—just resting in the arms of mother
nature.

At one of the liturgies we sang a song based on the prayer of St.
Francis of Assisi. Suleyman was moved by the words and asked for
a copy of the prayer. I found a copy, and a tape with the song on it. It
is a very ancient prayer, based on the hymn intoned by a thirteenth-
century monk who sang to mother nature, to the wolves and the
animals:

Lord, make me an instrument of your peace,
Where there is hatred, let me sow love;
where there is injury, pardon;
where there is doubt, faith;
where there is despair, hope;
where there is darkness, light;
and where there is sadness, joy.

Oh Divine Master, grant that I may not so much seek to be
consoled as to console;
to be understood as to understand;
to be loved as to love.

For it is in giving that we receive;
it is in pardoning that we are pardoned;
and it is in dying that we are born to eternal life.

When things seemed hopeless and the diffuse violence of the
system was suffocating Suleyman, I knew I could always refer to
this prayer and it would act like some northern light shimmering in
the dark. I had long talks with Suleyman about inner peace, both
up there in the north and then again, many times, in the city. I was
talking to myself as much as to him.

"Suleyman, the last and the only real space of freedom you have
is inside your head, inside your imagination and your heart. If you
let the uncles get inside your head, if you think about them day and
night, even if you win you have lost. You cannot let them inside
your head.

"The danger in such a long night is that you can become defined
by the struggle, by whom or what you are against. The danger is

that you will become like what you are fighting against."

I would like to have said this to the director of csis and to the many agents: you are becoming defined by the war against terror and you are becoming terrifying in the process.

Know who or what you are fighting for, what you treasure, what you value.

• • •

There is a time when it is morning before it is morning; when you can hear the morning before you see it. This is the moment when the birds begin to sound, slightly. And you know the difference between night and day is not so vast.

On May 18, 2006, Suleyman Goven received a letter from Immigration Canada indicating that he had been granted permanent resident status: "Although your application has taken some time . . ."

"Some time"—some thirteen years after he had been accepted as a refugee in Canada. That's some time, some long time.

The official government permanent resident status did nothing to stop continued harassment by csis officers. On September 7, 2006, the day that Suleyman finally held the landed immigrant document in his hand, he wrote a letter to the manager of the Canada Immigration office in Etobicoke. He was upset because his efforts to help other refugees complete their applications for refugee status were being used against him.

> The most recent attempts by csis to discredit me have involved attempting to coerce refugees into making statements that I have been fabricating refugee claims on their behalf. After I launched a civil suit against csis, csis escalated such attempts.

According to my information, CSIS has been telling claimants that they will be landed as a reward for admitting that their claims have been fabricated by me, but that absent such admission, their claims will be held in limbo for many years to come. This is tantamount to blackmail. In addition CSIS is attempting to recruit informants in my community to discredit my civil suit and to incriminate me. . . . You have caused untold misery to me, and no doubt to many other innocent refugees caught up in a system without appropriate checks and balances, and without justice.

This letter was never answered. Still the struggle with Someone, No One, continued. At least two or three times a year Suleyman learned that yet another Kurd had been questioned about the PKK and Suleyman's involvement in it.

Finally, on March 25, 2009, two and a half years after Suleyman had been landed, I wrote a letter to the chair of the Security Intelligence Review Committee. By that point almost nine years had passed since the Rae report had so painstakingly come to the conclusion that Suleyman Goven was an innocent person who had been unjustly accused of being a terrorist. Nevertheless, I wrote, CSIS was continuing to harass Suleyman Goven, and the harassment had intensified after Suleyman had filed the civil suit for damages.

"It is clear that SIRC could at least investigate this ongoing injustice. However, if SIRC only has the power to 'recommend' that CSIS change its actions, then it could become another exercise in futility and a waste of taxpayer money.

"I am writing to ask you honestly whether SIRC can do anything about this situation. We owe it to the reputation of SIRC, to the effectiveness of CSIS, to the integrity of Mr. Goven and to the integrity of this country to answer this question honestly. We also owe the tax-payers of Canada the assurance that the oversight of security agencies is effective."

In the following months I had telephone conversations and a brief correspondence with the Senior Counsel for SIRC, Sylvie Roussel. She said that Suleyman Goven had a right to make a second complaint to SIRC—that is, a complaint about the harassment that was continuing to take place. The Sanctuary Coalition discussed this option over a period of weeks, and I had a long conversation about it with Suleyman. We concluded, sadly, that it was pointless to make a second complaint because SIRC had no effective power and authority over CSIS. *In short, the watchdog had no teeth.* This toothless situation was not the fault of anyone on the SIRC staff or committee. The problem was in the legislation, which limited the powers of SIRC. The power to recommend is no power at all.

Thus, this book.

And thus it will be sent to as many members of Parliament as possible. And thus it will be read by those who "stand on guard for thee."

• • •

As his form of resistance Suleyman also took up even more writing. He became the founding editor of *Yeni Hayat*, a monthly newspaper that publishes articles not just in the Turkish and Kurdish languages but also in English, French, and very occasionally Arabic. The first issue of the paper appeared in February 2007. Suleyman writes a regular column and contributes pieces for the paper's website. He also became an excellent photographer.

In 2008, in a ceremony at Queen's Park, Suleyman received an award from the National Ethnic Press and Media Council of Canada for producing the best ethnic newspaper in the province. In fall 2009 the National Ethnic Press and Media Council recognized Suleyman and the newspaper in the category of "Editorial and Free Expression." He was elected vice-president of the Council and used his new credentials to cover significant political events. Suleyman, our friendly local terrorist, was photographed with Prime Minister Stephen Harper, Immigration Minister Jason Kenney, and the Liberal Party Leader of the Opposition, Michael Ignatieff.

One of his first columns for *Yeni Hayat* was entitled "My Militant Grandmother." In it he paid tribute to Rita Leddy, who had stood by him in the courtroom until her cancer made it impossible for her to attend.

Some three years later he wrote a column about Canada's gold medal in hockey at the Vancouver Olympics. A group of people involved in working with refugees, including Suleyman, had gathered at the Romero House centre on Bloor Street on that famous Sunday afternoon, February 28, 2010, to watch the hockey game between Canada and the United States. With an LCD projector enlarging the action, it was almost like having front-row seats to the game. Suleyman was sitting behind me and I could hear his voice throughout the game, although I could not see him. We were all clapping and yelling, alternately elated and dejected as the game played on. After Canada's Sidney Crosby scored the winning goal in overtime and the festivities began, we joined with the crowd in the stadium as they sang our national anthem, "O Canada."

I thought I could hear Suleyman singing . . .

MANUFACTURING "TERRORISTS":
REFUGEES, NATIONAL SECURITY, AND CANADIAN LAW

Sharryn J. Aiken

Introduction

ALTHOUGH numerous states and movements have used violence to achieve specific political goals throughout history, the use of the word "terrorism" has relatively recent origins. The term was coined to describe a specific phase of the French Revolution known as the Reign of Terror, when the Jacobins initiated a campaign of repression in which at least 17,000 French citizens were guillotined and many thousands more imprisoned and tortured. In this context, Mitchell indicates, "Terrorism was perceived as an unspeakable crime—the product of moral depravity or madness."[1] "Terrorism" was initially described as an exercise of repression by a state against its own citizens, but during the course of the nineteenth and twentieth centuries both the term itself and the measures adopted by states in response to it became increasingly politicized. One need only consider the U.S. description of its retaliatory bombing attacks in Sudan and Afghanistan as "counterterrorism," or the speeches of Israeli leaders decrying the "terrorist" acts of Palestinians while justifying gunfire on crowds of Palestinian civilians as "defence," to appreciate how "terrorists" are manufactured for the most cynical and explicitly political purposes.

Canadian officials acknowledge that Canada has never been a major target for "terrorist" attacks.[2] The government's preoccupation with "terrorism" has focused primarily on the perceived "terrorist" threat posed by refugees and immigrants arriving from non-Western countries. Security intelligence reports confirm the existence of individuals and organizations operating in Canada to support, plan, and mount attacks elsewhere, although open information by no means suggests that the participation rate of immigrants in these activities is proportionally higher than of people born in Canada.[3] Such reports have been used to justify a complex web of immigration security measures. While few would dispute the legitimacy of genuine efforts to protect public safety, the problem with many of these measures is that they have cast an unacceptably wide and uneven net. The "terrorist" has become the postmodern substitute for the "vicious class" that nineteenth-century immigration laws constructed as a tool of immigration control. In common with their historical counterpart, anti-terrorism provisions in the Immigration Act serve as a cover to legalize the broadest discretion over who gets in and who is permitted to stay.

In 1991 Gorlick commented that the government used its national security policies to exclude those considered to harbour ideological or political views inimical to the liberal democratic values of the Canadian state.[4] In the post–Cold War context with its attendant international realignments, this observation no longer provides a full account of immigration security policy. An analysis of current deportation practices suggests that immigration measures aimed at protecting the "security of Canada" are not about rooting out foes of democracy and genuine threats to the nation. They are but one tool, in an increasingly sophisticated arsenal, to contain and manage refugee admissions.[5] In this regard, not all refugee communities are subjected to the same level of security scrutiny.

As Whitaker explains in his recent discussion of the security dimension of refugee policy, the "systematic political bias of the Cold War has been replaced by a patchwork of specific biases." He points out that the injustices against individuals are just as frequent today, but the "biases are more diffuse." Indeed, under the new order, the designation of certain refugees as "terrorists" serves multiple geopolitical and economic interests. While I agree with Whitaker that racism should not be seen as a sole explanation for government security policy, current policies do reinforce systemic racism in Canadian law and practice.[6]

For example: on the one hand, the government introduced expedited screening and emergency evacuation for 5,000 ethnic Albanians fleeing Kosovo in 1999, in spite of the reasonably high level of active support for the Kosovo Liberation Army among the refugee population; on the other hand, there was an extremely modest, and belated, response to the humanitarian crisis of the 1990s in Sierra Leone, a country that for a decade suffered a devastating war producing a massive outflow of refugees. In another inherent contradiction, government policy permits certain diasporic communities to raise funds in support of political causes and organizations in their homelands with impunity, while other communities risk expulsion from Canada for the very same conduct. In November 2000 the Canadian Council for Refugees noted: "Certain ethnic or national groups are particularly apt to be targeted for extra security checks. . . . Those who have been found inadmissible or have been kept waiting without a decision being made on a security-related provision include significant numbers of Iranians with some association with the Mojahaddin movement and Kurdish people."[7]

In effect, the immigration/national-security apparatus replicates an imperative of exclusion and restriction that pre-emptively and selectively casts some groups of refugees and other non-citizens as "terrorist," "alien," and "other"—people on the periphery whose claims for justice can be ignored.[8]

As Canadian law changes its conception of refugees from victims and survivors to fearsome "terrorists," political activism that is lawful for citizens becomes a basis for expelling non-citizens. The expression of support for a liberation struggle being waged in one's country of origin can be sufficient grounds to be designated a security risk. The Immigration Act accords the same treatment to the mastermind of a hijacking and the person who has raised money in Canada to support an orphanage in her war-ravaged homeland. Refugee claimants seeking asylum and Convention refugees applying for permanent residence may be subjected to security interviews that all too frequently resemble interrogations and for which the individuals arrive unprepared, having been given no notice of the purpose of the interview or their entitlement to be represented by counsel.[9] Most of the adverse information that the Canadian Security Intelligence Service (CSIS, or "the Service") collects will be classified on national security grounds and therefore not disclosed to the person concerned. Refugee claimants may be deemed ineligible to even initiate their claims and be divested of the right to a "post-claim review." Subsequent administrative proceedings very often leave individuals in a legal limbo while their files await review by department analysts. Once a "security certificate" has been issued, the decision of a single "designated" judge is considered conclusive proof of the allegations against the individual and cannot be appealed. The result will be mandatory detention, followed ultimately by deportation back to the country where the refugee may be at serious risk of persecution, torture, or death. While the numbers of affected individuals are relatively small, the gravity of the issues at stake signals an urgent need for law reform.

"Terrorism": International Initiatives and Contemporary Discourse

The first international initiative aimed at combating "terrorism" was undertaken in 1937 by the League of Nations. The proposed Convention for the Prevention and Punishment of Terrorism defined "terrorism" as "criminal acts directed against a State and intended or calculated to create a state of terror in the minds of particular persons, or a group of persons or the general public." Only one nation, India, ratified the Convention before the outbreak of the Second World War and the demise of the League of Nations.[10] In the post–1945 era, the threat of "terrorism" gained increasing prominence on the agendas of the United Nations, and a number of Western states in particular. Between 1968 and 1972 a series of high-profile hijacking incidents against Israeli and Jordanian aircraft, together with the Munich Olympics attack by the Black September organization, coalesced international concern.[11] At the same time, recognition of the legitimacy of anti-colonial (and sometimes violent) struggles against oppressive regimes (for example, South Africa, Mozambique, and Palestine) was becoming increasingly important throughout the Third World. Through a series of U.N. resolutions the abstract principle of self-determination as initially articulated in the U.N. Charter was upgraded to an "invocable" right of peoples. This development culminated in the Decolonisation Declaration of 1960 and in the identical Article 1 of the International Covenants of Human Rights of 1966, which provided that "All peoples have the right to self-determination." As well, the 1970 Declaration of Principles of International Law Governing Friendly Relations among States accorded firm recognition to the principle of self-determination.[12]

In this context, any effort to define "terrorism" was fraught with difficulty. As Higgins noted, "If the West was nervous that a definition of terrorism could be used to include 'state terrorism', the third world was nervous that any definition which emphasized non-State actors would fail to differentiate between terrorism properly so called, and the struggle for national liberation."[13] When the draft Convention on the Prevention of Terrorism, sponsored by the United States, was introduced at the United Nations in 1972, a bitter debate ensued between First World and Third World nations on the merits of a categorical ban on the use of violence. The draft Convention was rejected. The United Nations attempted to achieve a fine balance between these competing concerns through a series of strongly worded resolutions condemning "all acts, methods and practices of terrorism" on the one hand and, on the other, by promulgating treaties that deliberately avoided umbrella definitions in favour of proscribing specific and defined criminal misconduct. Developments in international humanitarian law represent a parallel response to the question of national liberation wars.

By 2001 the United Nations had developed eleven separate agreements prohibiting, among other things, aircraft hijacking, aircraft sabotage, attacks against ships and fixed platforms in the ocean, attacks at airports, violence against officials and diplomats, hostage-taking, the use of unmarked plastic explosives, terrorist bombings (excluding, in certain cases, activities committed within a single state), and, in 1991, the financing of terrorist offences.

Regional bodies had adopted similar agreements. The essential goal of the treaties is to elevate the specified offences to the status of "international crimes," ensuring prosecution of the accused by imposing upon signatory states the alternative obligation to extradite or submit the accused for prosecution to the appropriate national authority. The new International Criminal Court (ICC), a separate but complementary initiative, will have jurisdiction over international crimes including genocide, crimes against humanity, war crimes, and aggression—whether committed by states or insurgent groups. However, the Rome Statute does not identify "terrorism" among the distinct categories of crimes within the court's jurisdiction. With the exception of the crime of aggression, which remains undefined, pending adoption of an agreed definition, the treaty defines each of the crimes with specific reference to illegal acts.[14] The Rome Statute includes detailed provisions for individual and "superior" criminal responsibility. In this regard, under the Rome Statute mere membership in an organization—in the absence of a nexus to the omission of an offence, or in the case of superior officers, in the absence of personal command responsibility for their sub-ordinates who committed an offence—is not a crime.

The inability of states to arrive at a consensus on the meaning of the term has not prevented international bodies from condemning "terrorism," nor has it prevented states from criminalizing specific acts. The 1996 Group of 8 Ministerial Conference on Terrorism adopted a series of measures that made no attempt to define terror-ism. Instead the agreed text aimed at facilitating extradition arrange-ments and clamping down on criminal use of the Internet and "camouflage" charities involved in illicit transborder fundraising. Before the meeting, President Clinton identified terrorism as "the greatest security challenge of the twenty-first century. . . . We can-not have economic security in a global economy unless we can stand against those forces of terrorism. The U.S. will lead the way and we expect our allies to walk with us hand in hand."[15]

In more concrete terms, Canada's Criminal Code identifies dis-crete offences involving aircraft, international maritime navigation, internationally protected persons, nuclear material, and hostage-taking, as well as war crimes and crimes against humanity, all of which may be subject to Canadian prosecution, regardless of where the offence was committed.[16] The Crimes against Humanity Act (2000) ensures that refugees who have committed such crimes may be subject to domestic prosecution. On the other hand, member-ship in an organization has not been a crime in Canada since the imposition of the War Measures Act in October 1970. A minority of countries, including Italy, Portugal, and Turkey, have enacted legislation making it a crime for citizens and non-citizens alike to belong to a "terrorist" organization, to provide support or recruit for a "terrorist" organization. Domestic laws in Germany, the United

Kingdom, and the United States identify "terrorism" itself as a crime but include a precise definition of the term for the purpose of applying the law. The majority of countries responding to a Council of Europe survey in 1991 indicated that they had no special anti-terrorism legislation.[17]

While the academic literature on "terrorism" includes a proliferation of definitions, the consensus among many authors is that there is no universally or even generally accepted definition. Schmid reports that 109 different definitions of the term "international terrorism" were advanced between 1936 and 1981, and more have appeared since.[18] Although there seems to be agreement that "terrorism" involves the threat or use of violence, Lambert indicates that differences in definition range from the semantic to the conceptual. According to Lacqueur the term has been used as a synonym for "rebellion, street battles, civil strife, insurrection, rural guerrilla war, coups d'état and a dozen other things," with the result that it has "become almost meaningless, covering almost any, and not necessarily political, act of violence." Levitt suggests that the effort to formulate a widely acceptable definition is akin to "the search for the Holy Grail." Commenting on the initiatives undertaken by the United Nations over the years, Higgins emphasizes, "Terrorism is a term without legal significance. . . . It is at once a shorthand to allude to a variety of problems with some common elements, and a method of indicating community condemnation for the conduct concerned." Commenting on the initial definition contained in the League of Nations Convention, Borricand observes that this initiative "has been much criticized and quite rightly so." He elaborates: "Indeed, defining terrorism by the terror it causes is a tautology; speaking of criminal acts is remarkably vague, since the notion of crime varies from one State to another; and lastly, classing as terrorism only those acts that are directed at a State . . . is a very restrictive idea. "[19]

In the face of this definitional quagmire, the use of "terrorist" as a conceptual category in the absence of any qualification of constituent elements must be seen for what it is: a highly charged political position embedded in the particularity of a given cultural, social, and tactical context.[20] In support of this thesis Chomsky identifies the political filters employed to cast the Kurds as "marxist and terrorist," while characterizing the Turkish state as a "secular democracy beleaguered by terrorism."[21] Challenging the definitions of "terrorism" exploited by the "terrorism industry" of Western states, quasi-private institutes, and private security firms, Herman and O'Sullivan assert:

> If . . . the West has been able to label the world's rebels in Indochina, Indonesia, the Philippines, South Africa, Central America, and other places as "terrorists," and the West and its proxies as engaging in "counterterror," this is a propaganda achievement of historic dimensions. It is also the ultimate Orwellian transformation: the victims are made the terrorists, whereas the terrorists are the alleged victims driven to a counterterror response.[22]

In a similar vein, Falk underscores the extent to which the language of "terrorism" has been enlisted in the service of partisan causes that lie at the root of contemporary geopolitics. When Western states criminalize popular movements that have been banned by ruling elites in their countries of origin, very often the main patterns of conflict are actually reinforced.[23] Support for Falk's analysis is found in two recent examples. External support became a critical component of the ANC's ultimate success in overthrowing the apartheid regime in South Africa. On the other hand, when the United States proscribed the Liberation Tamils of Tamil Eelam (LTTE) as a "foreign terrorist organization" in 1997, the prospects for initiating peace talks and bringing an end to the protracted war in Sri Lanka deteriorated. It is interesting to contrast the response of a spokesperson for the Sri Lankan foreign office, hailing the U.S. ban on the LTTE as "a victory for Sri Lanka's foreign policy," with the concern expressed by moderate critics that the U.S. policy would thwart attempts to bring the movement into the democratic mainstream, forcing it to become more intransigent.[24] When Western counter-terrorism policies quell all prospects for external dissent, fundraising, and mobilization, legitimate liberation struggles are further marginalized, leaving even less space for non-violent, political strategies.

The adage that often crystallizes the problem of defining "terrorism" is "One person's freedom-fighter is another's terrorist." The context of the international debate has been limited to non-state actors. Even the most recent treaties on the suppression of terrorist bombings and financing are directed narrowly at activities committed against states and their populations, but not by states. In this regard, Chadwick notes that the language used in efforts toward anti-terrorist codification is a manifestation of ideological solidarity on the part of some Western states. She asserts:

> States have yet to target themselves for codified sanction for acts of terrorism, whether such acts are state-sponsored, state supported, or state-conducted. This omission is particularly egregious when viewed in the light of the many state mechanisms of

public control which may work to provoke societal violence. This disregard of at least one-half of the equation required to solve the problem of political violence makes it highly possible that state-centric solutions arrived at are in error in both approach and effect.[25]

For Chadwick the problem is not the intrinsic nature of the term "terrorism," but rather the offence-specific and piecemeal nature of the U.N. treaties. While acknowledging the conceptual and definitional pitfalls, she advocates a more even-handed working definition of "terrorist offence," which stipulates that "the instigators of terrorist violence can be an individual, a group, or a government."[26] The crucial difference between Chadwick and the primarily Western "experts" and defenders of "terrorism" discourse, whom Chomsky and Falk sharply rebuke,[27] is that Chadwick focuses squarely on the need for an international strategy that accounts for and accommodates the legal rights and entitlements of "peoples" engaged in wars of national liberation.[28] Chadwick, in common with a broad range of other scholars, argues that the guidance of international humanitarian law is critical in any assessment of "terrorism," and ultimately in any effort to deter its occurrence.[29] When acts of "terror" and violence are committed in an armed conflict, international humanitarian law furnishes the rules of conduct for both state and non-state actors and distinguishes between permissible and impermissible uses of force.[30]

While critical theorists continue to interrogate the broader project of international law and its colonial antecedents, there is much less controversy about the pragmatic utility of using universal rules to define the categories of permissible participants and strategies involved in armed conflict. As noted by Greenwood, even before 1899, "the requirement that certain humanitarian principles be observed in warfare was well established in all main cultures."[31] According to norms that many scholars assert have achieved the status of customary international law, groups that can be identified as a "people" are entitled to use armed force to assert claims of self-determination against a state that engages in systematic repression and human rights violations. In such conditions an otherwise internal or civil conflict is "internationalized."[32] Falk indicates:

> There is no right to resort to force so long as a government behaves democratically and in fundamental accordance with the basic principles of human rights. But, where a government is oppressive toward a racial or political, ethnic minority or religious minority, or to a constituent people within its sovereignty . . . there is an increasing international recognition of the right to armed resistance.[33]

In effect, this is an extension of the principle of self-defence that legitimized the use of force by states against non-state actors, subject to the underlying causes of the conflict.[34]

In Canada, the Geneva Conventions Act directly implements our treaty commitments, and the government has been an advocate of the principles of equal rights and self-determination of peoples at the United Nations.[35] Acts of violence, no matter how deserving the ultimate goal, underscore the philosophical conundrum of means versus ends and whether it can ever be ethical to sanction death and destruction in support of a just cause. It is difficult, if not deeply problematic from a moral perspective, to justify the deliberate killing of an unarmed population, regardless of the cause or purpose. In this regard, international humanitarian law does not seek to justify or rationalize violence, but rather to assert a comprehensive set of rules that apply to all actors in a conflict—and to promote the prosecution of those who violate the rules clearly and consistently. A claim to "combatant status" does not immunize all acts of violence, but it has a significant impact on the characterization of particular actors and offences. In the context of wars of liberation or independence being waged by groups with a recognized right to self-determination, the use of force against military targets or police units empowered to conduct "public order" missions is permitted. When civilians are targeted in attacks by such groups, those acts are subject to sanction as violations of humanitarian law, with recourse to a set of well-established defences. Thus illicit acts of war perpetrated by or on behalf of "peoples" struggling for their rights to self-determination are a separable phenomenon distinct from individual, sporadic acts of violence in peacetime.

Article 21 of the 1999 treaty on the financing of "terrorism" explicitly acknowledges the interplay between its own mandate and international humanitarian law: "Nothing in this Convention shall affect other rights, obligations and responsibilities of States and individuals under international law, in particular the purposes of the Charter of the United Nations, international humanitarian law and other relevant conventions."[36] Thus full compliance with the treaty would explicitly require its provisions to be interpreted in light of international humanitarian law. . . . The treaty is especially relevant to the Canadian context, because a majority of the refugees and other non-citizens considered security risks under the Immigration Act are not people who have ever engaged in violent activity themselves, but are associated with Canadian organizations that csis has identified as "fronts" for fundraising in support of "homeland conflicts."[37]

Arguably, domestic law concerning conspiracy, common intention, and aiding or abetting unlawful acts already addresses the situation of people who contribute material support to the commission of illegal acts. While any individual in Canada could be subject to criminal prosecution on these grounds, in practice, prosecutions are never initiated against refugees whom the government finds to be engaged in financing "terrorism." The fact that these refugees have not engaged in any unlawful activities (either in Canada or their country of origin) must be at least a partial explanation for the absence of such prosecutions.[38] The U.N. treaty itself criminalizes "terrorist" fundraising only to the extent that funds are collected "wilfully . . . with the intention that they should be used or in the knowledge that they are to be used, in full or in part, in order to carry out" the specified offences or acts. Additional provisions indicate that it is also an offence to participate as an accomplice, organize or direct others to commit an offence, or intentionally "contribute to the commission of an offence by a group of persons acting with a common purpose."[39] The treaty is a clear affirmation that those who financially contribute to violent acts are to be considered just as culpable as those who detonate the bombs.

However, the treaty's provisions clearly articulate the legal requirement of *mens rea*. Individuals will be found complicit in the commission of an offence only when they knew or ought to have known that their activities were supporting the crime. The requirement of this mental element is consistent with the standards widely applied in both criminal and refugee law and necessarily implies that mere membership or affiliation with groups responsible for international crimes would not be sufficient to establish an offence under the treaty.

Significantly, the treaty incorporates an express limitation on the duty to extradite offenders who will be subjected to discriminatory applications of the criminal law authority:

> Nothing in this Convention shall be interpreted as imposing an obligation to extradite . . . if the requested State Party has substantial grounds for believing that the request for extradition . . . has been made for the purpose of prosecuting or punishing a person on account of that person's race, religion, nationality, ethnic origin or political opinion or that compliance with the request would cause prejudice to that person's position for any of these reasons.[40]

As Hathaway emphasizes, an individual does not face genuine criminal prosecution where discrimination results in selective prosecution, denial of procedural or adjudicative fairness, or differential punishment.[41] The treaty further stipulates that its measures must be implemented through the mechanism of domestic criminal law. In Canada the necessary result would be that anyone alleged to have been involved in financing "terrorism" will be afforded all the safeguards of the criminal justice system, including constitutionally protected rights to counsel, to know and meet and the state's case, and most importantly, the benefit of the criminal law standard of proof—not to be convicted unless guilt is established beyond a reasonable doubt.

Canadian Immigration Law and National Security

Canada's historical record clearly reflects the extent to which each new influx of immigrants engendered reactions that sought to criminalize foreigners and thwart others from gaining admission in the first place. As Stasiulus and Yuval-Davis observe, immigration laws have been used in settler societies to encourage "desirable" immigrants to settle in the country and to exclude "undesirable" ones.[42] In this regard, post-Confederation immigration law and policy in Canada share a trajectory with other colonial states. While seeking to promote immigration as a strategy essential for industrial growth, the newly formed Confederation was equally concerned about controlling entry and safeguarding the developing nation from individuals thought undesirable because of their "race" or nationality, as well as for economic, medical, criminal, or security reasons.

Canada's first Act Respecting Immigration and Immigrants, passed in 1869, was designed primarily to ensure the safety and protection of British immigrants travelling to Canada. As early as 1872, there was a prohibition against immigrants who might be a security risk. That year an amendment to the Immigration Act provided that "The Governor in Council may, by proclamation, whenever he deems it necessary, prohibit the landing in Canada of any criminal, or other vicious class of immigrants, to be designated by such proclamation." Section 41 of the Immigration Act of 1910 added to the prohibited classes "any person other than a Canadian citizen [who] advocates in Canada the overthrow by force or violence of the Government of Great Britain or Canada, or other British Dominion, Colony, possession or dependency, or the overthrow by force or violence of constitutional law or authority." A privative clause in the Immigration Act denied the right of appeal to anyone who was refused admission or ordered deported pursuant to the Act.[43]

In the wake of the Russian Revolution of 1917, the "Red Scare" in the West, and increasing labour unrest in Canada, the scope of Section 41 was widened to include anyone who "advocates or teaches the unlawful destruction of property" and anyone who "is a member of or affiliated with any organization entertaining or teaching the disbelief in organized government." The government used this statutory authority to bar entry or deport hundreds of "anarchists and revolutionaries," who were primarily suspected communists and union organizers.[44] This amendment gave the government the right to deport anyone who was deemed a member of one of the inadmissible classes, for up to five years after arrival in Canada. By 1923 all immigrants were required to have visas, and procedures for the examination of visa applicants began to develop. During the interwar period and through World War II, the Immigration Act continued to provide government officers with broad discretionary powers to exclude individuals, including "enemy aliens," on the grounds of national security.

Following World War II, the Canadian government sought to expand the immigration program in an effort to meet labour-market demands and contribute to the relief of displaced persons in Europe. In recognition of the security problem posed by the surge in immigration, the RCMP was dispatched to London to join the immigration vetting team. In the immediate postwar period, fear of Soviet infiltration (not Nazi collaborators) was the primary security concern. This concern became heightened when a clerk from the Soviet Embassy named Gouzenko defected and revealed the existence of a communist spy network. The "Gouzenko affair" generated a widespread preoccupation within government about security—a concern that grew as Cold War tensions increased.

Immigration regulations continued the absolute prohibition on admission of communists, while Cabinet directives authorized a selective course of immigration security screening without deciding whom to screen, how to screen, or what screening criteria would be applied. These decisions were left to the discretion of the RCMP. Records indicate that Cabinet regarded security matters as a key priority but did not want the security process made public. As reported in a 1998 Federal Court decision, "Not only was the actual process secret but the fact that such a process was in place was a closely guarded secret."[45]

In 1952 a new Immigration Act was implemented, governing Canadian immigration procedures for the following twenty-five years. Section 5 of the Act listed the classes of persons who were prohibited from admission to Canada, while Section 19 provided the authority to deport those already in Canada on security grounds. According to the Act, individuals were considered security risks who are, have been, or are likely to become "members of or associated with any organization, group or body of any kind concerning which there are reasonable grounds for believing that it promotes or advocates . . . subversion by force or other means." Other subsections of the Act specifically addressed related security risks, including espionage, sabotage, and treason. The Immigration Appeal Board Act of 1967 implemented a right of appeal for people facing deportation but also set out the conditions for overriding appeal procedures in serious security cases.[46] From its early roots through to the 1960s, the explicit objective of immigration law and policy was to sustain the British character of Canada and exclude those who were thought incapable of contributing to the government's assimilationist project of nation-building. The driving force behind measures of national security and immigration control during this period was the Anglo-Saxon fear that the influx of foreigners threatened the nation's "racial purity" and/or political fabric.[47]

Canada became a party to the 1951 United Nations Convention on the Status of Refugees (Refugee Convention) in 1969. The Convention carved out an explicit exception to the notion that states had the absolute prerogative to decide whom to admit to their territories.[48] Qualified refugees would no longer be seeking a privilege, but asserting a right that statutory states would be obliged to consider. Despite the idealism and neutral language embedded in the Convention, ideological considerations frequently informed Canada's response to international refugee crises, particularly in the early years of the Cold War. The refuge provided to people fleeing communist regimes in Hungary in 1956, Czechoslovakia in 1968, and Vietnam in 1979, in contrast to the relatively closed door offered to Chilean refugees fleeing Pinochet's coup in 1973, is a striking manifestation of this tendency.[49]

In response to a government green paper recommending that immigration legislation embody a more positive approach, a new Immigration Act was implemented in 1976.[50] This legislation was amended several times over the following two decades. For the first time the objectives of Canada's immigration policy were explicitly spelled out. These included attainment of Canada's demographic goals, promotion of family reunification, and development of a strong economy. The Act included among its purposes the imposition of standards of admission that do not discriminate on grounds of race, national, or ethnic origin, colour, religion, or sex; the fulfilment of Canada's international legal obligations to refugees and upholding its humanitarian tradition toward the displaced and the persecuted; the maintenance and protection of the health, safety, and good order of Canadian society, and promotion of international order and justice by denying the use of Canadian territory to persons who are likely to engage in criminal activity. The Act incorporated the essential parts of the 1951 Convention definition of a refugee and its "exclusion clauses." Protection would be afforded to persons with a well-founded fear of persecution for reasons of race, religion, nationality, or membership in a particular social group or political opinion. Status would be denied to those not deserving protection, including the perpetrators of war crimes, serious non-political crimes, and acts "contrary to the purposes and principles of the United Nations." The Act also incorporated the principle of *non-refoulement*, the positive commitment not to remove refugees to a country where their life or freedom would be threatened for any of the Convention reasons. Exceptions, consistent with the Refugee Convention, were stipulated for persons who constituted a danger to "the security of Canada" or public safety.

Section 19(1) of the Act established a somewhat refined list of classes of people who were inadmissible to Canada for security reasons: persons for whom there are "reasonable grounds to believe" that they have engaged or will engage in espionage, subversion against democratic government, and subversion by force of any government. In addition, persons were inadmissible where "there are reasonable grounds to believe [they] will engage in acts of violence that would or might endanger the lives or safety of persons in Canada or are members of or likely to participate in the unlawful activities of an organization that is likely to engage in such acts of violence."[51]

Finally, there was a provision to exclude persons who had committed war crimes and crimes against humanity.[52] The Act explicitly referred to the Criminal Code for the purposes of defining war crimes and crimes against humanity, and the Code's definitions of "public order offences" would clearly be relevant to the interpretation of espionage. However, nothing in the new Act, regulations, or administrative policy provided any criteria or guidance for what constituted "membership" or "subversion." Over the next decade, Canada opened its doors to thousands of refugees from nontraditional source countries. However, Canada's record of compliance with international human rights standards and the Refugee Convention in particular continued to be uneven.[53]

In the wake of concerns about the conduct of the Security Service of the RCMP in the 1970s, the government established the Commission of Inquiry Concerning Certain Activities of the RCMP commonly referred to by the name of its chair, Mr. Justice D.C. McDonald. In 1981 the McDonald Commission released its second report, *Freedom and Security under the Law.* The Commission found that the RCMP had subjected many groups, including the "new left," Quebec separatists, unions, the Indian movement, and others to surveillance, infiltration, and "dirty tricks," solely on the grounds that they were exercising their freedom of expression through lawful advocacy, protest, and dissent. A full chapter of the Commission's report addressed immigration security screening. The Commission found that the statutory security criteria set out in the Immigration Act were "too broad" and inconsistent with the definition of "threats to the security of Canada," which the Commission proposed should inform all security-related screening activities. The Commission observed:

> Canada must meet both the requirements of security and the requirements of democracy: we must never forget that the fundamental purpose of the former is to secure the latter. . . . In

taking the position that the requirements of security in Canada must be reconciled with the requirements of democracy, let us be clear that we regard responsible government, the rule of law and the right to dissent as among the essential requirements of our system of democracy.[54]

Although the Commission recommended including political violence and "terrorism" within the admissibility provisions of the Immigration Act, it underscored the importance of distinguishing between international groups secretly pursuing in Canada their terrorist objectives against foreign governments, from representatives of foreign liberation or dissident groups who come to Canada to promote their cause openly.[55] Based on the Commission's findings, Parliament endorsed the establishment of a new security intelligence agency, outside of the RCMP, with a mandate to investigate and advise but without prosecutorial or enforcement powers.

In 1984 the Canadian Security Intelligence Service Act was adopted, and the service was created to, among other things, provide government departments and agencies with security assessments on prospective immigrants. Section 2 of the CSIS Act defines "threats to the security of Canada" as being (1) espionage or sabotage; (2) foreign-influenced activities within or in relation to Canada that are detrimental to its interests and are clandestine or deceptive and involve a threat to any person; (3) activities within or relating to Canada, directed toward or in support of the threat or use of serious violence against persons or property for the purpose of achieving a political objective within Canada or a foreign state; and (4) activities directed against undermining by covert unlawful acts—or directed toward or intended ultimately to lead to the destruction or overthrow by violence of—the constitutionally established system of government in Canada.

The statutory language in Section 2 is very broad and has been the subject of criticism for this reason. As Gorlick notes, statutory terms such as "clandestine" or "deceptive" and "foreign influenced" are not defined in the Act, and "inevitably the interpretation of such terms will fall to the agency that has the most to gain from statutory power, that is, CSIS itself."[56] An important safeguard, however, is the inclusion at the end of Section 2 of the specific qualification that a threat to the security of Canada "does not include lawful advocacy, protest or dissent unless carried on in conjunction with any of the activities referred to above."[57]

Parliament failed to implement the McDonald Commission's proposals on revising the Immigration Act. The result is that the definition used by CSIS officers to investigate and provide advice to ministers on security risks that may be posed by prospective immigrants continues to be inconsistent with the admissibility provisions of the Immigration Act. Whereas the term "threat" in the CSIS Act is specifically defined in terms of enumerated activities rather than associations, the Immigration Act maintained its use of broad admissibility categories. Over the next decade many of the criticisms surfaced that had been levelled against the RCMP, and now were directed at the new security intelligence agency and the practices and conduct of its officers.[58]

Complaints have been made to the Security Intelligence Review Committee (SIRC), the agency "watchdog" for CSIS, documenting the extent to which the service has crossed the line and is engaging not just in monitoring threats to the security of Canada, but, like the RCMP before it when dealing with "subversives," is intruding into the lives and futures of those involved in legitimate forms of expression and dissent.[59] Reporting on investigations spanning several years, SIRC found instances in which CSIS instructions that sources report on only "authorized subjects of an investigation" had not been fully implemented. Also noted was "an occasional lack of rigour in the Service's application of existing policies, which oblige it to weigh the requirement to protect civil liberties against the need to investigate potential threats."[60] Media reports have exposed how, in some cases, refugees have been overtly or implicitly induced to become informers on fellow community members—with promises of prompt resolution of their own residence applications.[61] All prospective immigrants, including refugees, are under a certain compulsion to co-operate with CSIS officers because a positive recommendation from the Service is a condition for obtaining permanent residence status and citizenship.

Canada signed the 1984 Convention Against Torture (CAT) in 1985 without any reservation and ratified it in 1987, after extensive consultations with provincial and territorial governments.[62] Article 3 of the CAT imposes an absolute, non-derogable obligation on states not to return anyone to a country where she or he is at risk of torture, effectively superseding the security exception in the Refugee Convention. Although the government was an increasingly vocal proponent of human rights standards and institutions in international and regional forums, no steps were taken to incorporate the obligations assumed under Article 3 of the CAT into domestic immigration law. In the same period, the government was setting up the Immigration and Refugee Board, which would provide refugee claimants with an oral hearing. A Supreme Court decision interpreting the new Charter of Rights and Freedoms held that existing administrative procedures for determining refugee status inside Canada failed to meet the procedural guarantees of fundamental justice.[63]

In 1992, as Cold-War security considerations gave way to an increasing preoccupation with deterring "illegal migration" from the South, the Canadian government introduced a series of restrictive amendments to the Immigration Act. Bill C-86 made changes to the overall structure of existing immigration security procedures and enumerated a set of specific objectives for the scheme under the heading "Safety and Security of Canada." Section 38.1 of the amended Act articulated the purposes of the security procedures:

> Recognizing that persons who are not Canadian citizens or permanent residents have no right to come into or remain in Canada and that permanent residents have only a qualified right to do so, and recognizing the necessity of cooperation with foreign governments and agencies in maintaining national security, the purposes of sections 39 to 40.2 are
>
> (a) to enable the Government of Canada to fulfil its duty to remove persons who constitute a threat to the security or interests of Canada or whose presence endangers the lives or safety of persons in Canada;
>
> (b) to ensure the protection of sensitive security and criminal intelligence information; and
>
> (c) to provide a process for the expeditious removal of persons found to be members of an inadmissible class referred to in section 39 or 40.1.[64]

Bill C-86 introduced a new form of criminality into the Act, provisions to render refugees and immigrants "inadmissible" where there are reasonable grounds to believe they will "engage in terrorism" or are "members of an organization that there are reasonable grounds to believe will . . . engage in terrorism." An additional subsection provided that persons are inadmissible if they have engaged in "terrorism," or are "members of an organization that was engaged in terrorism," unless they can satisfy the Minister that their admission would not be detrimental to the national interest.[65] According to former Solicitor General Doug Lewis, these clauses were designed to ensure that Canada does not become a safe haven for retired or active terrorists.[66] The subsections dealing with espionage and subversion were broadened to include within their ambit past or present membership in organizations that have engaged in these acts in the past, are engaging in them now, or will engage in them in the future.

The package of amendments also introduced "access criteria" into the Act, requiring all refugee claimants to undergo an eligibility determination pursuant to an enumerated list of disqualifications that were based, among other things, on the new security admissibility criteria. In cases where the Minister found it "contrary to the public interest," claimants would be divested of the right to pursue their refugee claim.[67] Subject to a further ministerial opinion that they constituted a "danger to the security of Canada," Convention refugees as well as those deemed ineligible to claim refugee status were to be deported back to the very countries from which they fled and where their lives or freedom would be threatened.[68] In defence of the legislative amendments, it was suggested that the former Immigration Act "put the safety and security of Canadians at risk . . . [and] we have to face the fact that the world of the 1990's is a world of increasingly sophisticated, internationally organized criminals and terrorists."[69]

Once the amendments contained in Bill C-86 were implemented, immigration officers had an expanded basis to support determinations of inadmissibility. With the new provisions on "terrorism," the

Immigration Act delegated the job of identifying possible terrorists to CSIS while retaining for its own department the ultimate authority to decide who will be excluded from Canada on the basis of possible links to "terrorism." Certain refugee communities found themselves increasingly subject to surveillance by CSIS. Long delays associated with security clearance procedures meant that some individuals could expect to wait years before being able to sponsor family members, enrol in post-secondary education, start a business, or travel outside the country. Complaints lodged with SIRC about these delays or the nature of advice provided by the Service failed to resolve the problems. In three Kurdish cases, SIRC Chairman Robert Rae concluded that adverse assessments provided by CSIS were based on inaccurate assumptions. Despite the extensive investigations and hearings that supported SIRC's conclusions in these cases, the Service responded by preparing "updated assessments" in defence of its original advice, a move that has been interpreted as an attempt to overrule and effectively discredit the committee.[70]

The absence of definition or discriminating content for the terms "terrorism," "membership in a terrorist organization," and "security of Canada" permits the Minister of Citizenship and Immigration unfettered discretion to issue security certificates. Unlike the procedures set up in the United Kingdom, where there are statutory definitions and the designation by the executive of which groups and organizations meet the definition is subject to approval by both Houses of Parliament and even appeal, there are no public procedures to deal with the designation of terrorist organizations.

By the 1990s there was an emerging consensus among scholars and legal experts that both the principle of *non-refoulement* and the prohibition against torture had become rules of customary international law, and further, peremptory norms of *jus cogens*.[71] In the extradition context, two Supreme Court rulings confirmed that fundamental justice should prevent Canada from surrendering a fugitive to a foreign state in circumstances in which that person would be subjected to torture. In the same spirit, in 1996 Canadian government representatives in Geneva joined in the consensus for the 1996 conclusion of the UNHCR's Executive Committee in reaffirming "the fundamental principle of *non-refoulement*, which prohibits the expulsion and return of persons in respect of whom there are grounds for believing that they would be in danger of being subjected to torture, as set forth in the Convention against Torture."[72]

Yet within the next two years the government executed deportation orders in direct contravention of requests by the United Nations Committee against Torture and the Inter-American Commission on Human Rights.[73] Domestically, the government was maintaining its firm commitment to its "right" to deport criminals and "security risks," regardless of the human rights at issue. Although a United Nations resolution urges states to ensure that refugee status is "not used for the purpose of preparing or organizing terrorist acts," international institutions firmly support an absolute prohibition against deporting anyone to a county where there is risk of torture. Removal is also proscribed to a country where fair trial guarantees are absent, the death penalty will be imposed (albeit with considerable variation in state practice in this regard), or, with some balancing of interests, in cases that result in statelessness, and family separation, particularly where children are involved.

Meanwhile, repeated calls have come from some quarters for Canada to restrict access to its refugee program, with an increasing public perception that Canada's "porous" borders are endangering

Canadians. In response to such concerns, the federal government commissioned a series of studies and consultations and proposed a number of wide-ranging reforms to the Immigration Act. Bill C-31, the Immigration and Refugee Protection Act, provides a good indication of future policy directions. As for national security issues, the bill maintained the provisions related to "membership" and "terrorism," with no definition or statutory criteria for either term. There was provision for discretionary relief in circumstances where the minister was "satisfied that the admission would not be detrimental to the national interest."[74] The bill failed to address repeated recommendations that the definition of "security threat" in the Act be harmonized with the definition in the CSIS Act.[75] In addition to proposing broader grounds for security inadmissibility, the bill proposed to treat permanent residents and other non-citizens in the same manner under a new category as "foreign nationals." Currently, permanent residents faced with security proceedings have automatic access to SIRC, which examines the basis of the security opinion and provides an important check on the authority of CSIS.

The SIRC counsel has an opportunity to question witnesses who have been permitted to testify *ex parte* and in effect represent the interests of the person concerned. A summary of such evidence, subject to security "expurgation," is provided. It is only after the hearing is completed that SIRC issues a recommendation to the Governor in Council on whether a certificate should be issued. In proceedings involving non-permanent residents, on the other hand, the certificate has already been issued, and the task of a "designated judge" (one of a small number of Federal Court judges who have received special clearance to review security cases) is to determine whether it should be quashed. The government's case is presented primarily in secret and in the absence of the person concerned. In most cases, the csis officers who actually conducted the interviews and tendered the adverse security recommendation are not made available for questioning. The court has no independent counsel to assist, nor are there any special rules governing the unique features of such hearings.[76] Bill C-31 proposed the lower standard of procedural justice for all foreign nationals by stripping sirc of its current responsibility for permanent residents. Both refugees and permanent residents were to be accorded only an "informal and expeditious" Federal Court review of ministerial security opinions, with no possibility of further review or appeal. In 1990 a parliamentary review of the csis Act had recommended that the Immigration Act be amended to allow *any* person subject to an adverse security report to have the case investigated by sirc, with direct recourse to an administrative hearing.[77] The latest legislative initiative not only failed to address the existing shortcoming in the Act, but was proposing to further erode an essential safeguard. Although the bill contained new references to the cat, the explicit exemption authorizing the Minister to deport people regardless of the risks they might face remained in place for designated security cases.[78]

The overhaul of the Immigration Act in 1978, implementation in 1982 of the Canadian Charter of Rights and Freedoms, as well as the emergence of new international standards, generated considerable optimism about the prospects for a meaningful amelioration of conditions for immigrants and refugees as historically disadvantaged groups in Canadian society. Recourse to "Charter challenges" would offer an important mechanism of accountability, with the courts providing aggrieved individuals direct access to public decisions affecting their lives and an opportunity to challenge laws independent of government law reform agendas.[79] Despite these lofty hopes, there has been little evidence of progress. The individuals and groups subject to security targeting may have changed, but the measures proposed in 2000 bear remarkable similarity to historical forms of exclusion. The enforcement of the seemingly neutral admissibility provisions and their attendant procedures leave wide scope for unprincipled and discriminatory decision with virtually no appeal mechanism and limited procedural rights. Resort to the courts has not addressed the inequities in the system but instead has frequently reinforced them.

This is a revised version of an article originally published in *Refuge: Canada's Periodical on Refugees*, vol. 19, no. 5 (2001).

Sharryn J. Aiken is an assistant professor in the Faculty of Law at Queen's University. The author gratefully acknowledges Barbara Jackman for her generosity and assistance. The author also thanks Janet Dench, Brian Gorlick, Audrey Macklin, and Lorne Sossin for their helpful comments on an earlier draft of the original article. This paper is dedicated to Sami Durgun and Suleyman Goven, whose struggles for justice in Canada remain an inspiration.

APPENDIX B

EXCERPT FROM THE SIRC "REPORT INTO THE COMPLAINT OF SULEYMAN GOVEN," BY THE HON. BOB RAE

File No.: 1500-83

April 3, 2000

IN THE MATTER OF A COMPLAINT UNDER SECTION 41 OF THE CANADIAN SECURITY INTELLIGENCE SERVICE ACT

Mr. Suleyman Goven, Complainant, and The Canadian Security Intelligence Service, Respondent

Dates of Hearing: September 15, 16, 23, 24, 25, 1998; October 9, 1998; November 10, 23, 1998; December 2, 21, 22, 1998; January 26, 27, 1999; February 1, 2, 1999

Place of Hearing: Toronto
Before: The Honourable Robert Keith Rae, P.C., Q.C.

VII. CONCLUSIONS

7.1 General Findings

7.1.1 Relevant History Concerning the PKK

When the allied forces broke up the Ottoman Empire in 1920, the Kurds were promised a state of their own: Kurdistan. The promise never materialized. "*Kurdistan*" was divided between Turkey and to a lesser extent between Iran, Iraq, Syria, and the former Soviet Union. Throughout this century, the Kurds have been subject to repression, especially in Turkey and Iraq. The precondition for equality under Turkey's constitution and laws is that the Turkish Kurds can enjoy the freedoms and rights guaranteed under that constitution to "all Turkish citizens" only if they deny their heritage.

Substantial evidence was presented to the Committee with respect to the treatment of the Kurdish minority in Turkey, including documentation from Amnesty International and Human Rights Watch. Turkish officials often argue that nearly one-fourth of the 450-seat Parliament is made up of "Turks of Kurdish origin." In reality, however, only those who deny their ethnic identity can actually participate. The persecution of anyone involved in Kurdish issues is also well documented. The case of several Kurdish M.P.s has been widely publicized in the West,[1] but it is not unique. Journalists working on newspapers related to the Kurdish issue have been reported missing, and the offices of newspapers and magazines have been bombed. Anyone writing about the Kurds risks persecution, torture, and death. There are also well-documented cases of academics, scientists, and writers in Turkish jails serving lengthy prison terms for their political views.

On April 12, 1995, representatives of Turkish Kurds, not allowed to voice their aspirations in Parliament, set up a Kurdish Parliament in Exile to further their effort for a peaceful solution. Kurdish M.P.s persecuted by Turkey, as well as representatives of the ERNK [Kurdistan National Liberation Front], are Members of that Parliament, currently based in Brussels and which was working on a major Kurdish National Congress Meeting. In 1999, Turkish authorities captured and arrested Abdullah (Apo) Ocalan, the leader of the PKK. After his arrest, he issued a strong denunciation of violence and terrorism, a position supported by leadership of the PKK. Ocalan has been convicted of crimes against the Turkish people and has been sentenced to death.

Among the major political movements in Kurdistan is the Partye Karkaran-e-Kurdistan or Kurdistan Workers' Party (known by its acronym PKK). It was officially founded by Abdullah (Apo) Ocalan in 1978 in Istanbul. It has emerged as the focal point of nationalist Kurdish resistance to Turkish rule in the past two decades.

The PKK has been both a military and political organization in Turkey. It carried on guerilla warfare and armed struggle in Turkey, and on Turkey's borders, until the capture of its leader Abdullah (Apo) Ocalan in the spring of 1999. It has carried out bombing activities in most of Turkey's major cities and in parts of Western Europe. The Service estimated that approximately 30,000 people have been killed in the PKK's struggle to obtain an autonomous Kurdish state.

Currently, the PKK consists of a main political body which is the Party itself. In effect, this body functions as its legislative arm while the Kurdistan National Liberation Front (ERNK)[2] and the Kurdistan National Liberation Army (ARGK) are its executive bodies. The overall political, social, and military apparatus of the organization is complex. Each function or activity is carried out by separate committees.

In reaching my conclusions on the issues, I have been guided by my review of the Service's documentation, the submission of both parties, the study of the case law, as well as the academic literature.

Notes

CHAPTER 2: HE WAS LEFT ALONE

1. *The World Guide 2003/2004: An Alternative Reference to the Countries of Our Planet* (London: New Internationalist Publications, 2003), p.540.

2. See David McDowall, *A Modern History of the Kurds*, 3rd rev. ed. (London: I.B. Tauris and Co., 2004). The Alevis are more dominant in Turkey, where they make up twenty-five million of the seventy million population.

3. See Multicultural Canada, "Kurds: Migration, Arrival, and Settlement" <multiculturalcanada.ca>.

4. A landed immigrant can get access to student loans, travel outside the country, and apply for loans. The term "landed immigrant," long in use, was officially replaced by the term "permanent resident" under the Immigration and Refugee Protection Act of 2002 (though it is still used in common parlance today). Having a permanent resident status is a requirement for becoming a citizen. Note that the government has since changed the law to allow those who have been accepted as Convention refugees (but who are not yet permanent residents) to have access to student loans.

5. The story of the Ontario Sanctuary Coalition and its intertwining history with Romero House is developed more fully in Mary Jo Leddy, *At the Border Called Hope: Where Refugees Are Neighbours* (Toronto: HarperCollins, 1997).

CHAPTER 3: ALL NIGHT

1. This chapter's account of the interview conducted by the Canadian Security and Intelligence Service was first published in Leddy, *At the Border Called Hope*, pp.73–82. It is slightly altered here in style but not in substance.

2. Later, in December 2002, the Canadian government did put the PKK on the list of banned terrorist groups as part of its omnibus anti-terrorism bill. By this time the leader of the PKK had been captured and the PKK had withdrawn most of its fighters from the southeastern corner of Turkey. In 2002 the PKK announced that it was ending its campaign of armed struggle and calls for an independent Kurdistan, and was now pushing for a political resolution to the Kurdish problem. The *Amnesty International Report: State of the World's Human Rights* (2009) entry for Turkey continues to report armed conflict between the government and PKK: <http://thereport.amnesty.org/en/regions/europe-central-asia/turkey>.

CHAPTER 4: AND HE STRUGGLED

1. Martin van Bruinessen, "Genocide in Kurdistan? The Suppression of the Dersim Rebellion in Turkey (1937-38) and the Chemical War against the Iraqi Kurds (1988)," in *Genocide: Conceptual and Historical Dimensions*, ed. George J. Andreopoulos (Philadelphia: University of Pennsylvania Press, 1994), p.145.

2. As usual the massacre figures vary widely according to the source. It would be a mistake to see this massacre as being perpetrated by all Turks. Many Turks and Kurds risked their lives trying to help the Armenians. See Amir Hassanpour, "Ninety Years Later: The Armeninan Genocide Continues," CTV.ca, April 24, 2005 <http://www.ctv.ca/generic/WebSpecials/armeian_genocide/ninety.html>.

3. Henry H. Riggs, *Days of Tragedy in Armenia: Personal Experiences in Harpoot 1915-1917* (Ann Arbor, Mich.: Gomidas Institute, 1997), p.111.

4. Van Bruinessen, "Genocide in Kurdistan?" p.145.

5. Cf. David Zeidan, "The Alevi of Anatolia," December 1995 <www.angel fire.com/az/rescon/ALEVI.html>. See also Zeidan, "The Alevi of Anato-

lia," *Middle East Review of International Affairs*, 3,4 (December 1999).

6. Mehrdad R. Izady, *The Kurds: A Concise History and Handbook* (Washington, D.C.: Taylor and Francis, 1992), p.62.

7. Frederico Allodi, "PTSD in Families and Victims of Forced Disappearance," paper delivered at the meeting of the Society for Traumatic Stress Studies, San Francisco, Oct. 27–30, 1989, p.2.

8. Frederico Allodi, "Humanism and Medical Science in the Prevention of Torture," paper delivered at the National Institute of Health, Bethesda, Md., April 14, 1986; Michael Brue et al., "Belief Systems as Coping Factors for Traumatized Refugees: A Pilot Study," *European Psychiatry*, vol. 17, issue 8 (December 2002), pp. 451–58.

9. See the terrorist group profile of TIKKO, National Consortium for the Study of Terrorism and Responses to Terrorism <http://www.start.umd.edu/start/data/tops/terrorist_organization_profile>. "Like most Turkish leftist groups, the TKP/ML-TIKKO couched its anti-government and anti-western rhetoric and activities within a broader socialist revolutionary context."

CHAPTER 5: THE FACELESS ONE

1. See Appendix B, section 7.1.1, "Relevant History Concerning the PKK," by the Hon. Bob Rae.

2. Something similar was happening to the Kurdish community in England and Germany. See William Clark, "Searching for Asylum," a review of "The Targeting and Criminalisation of Kurdish Asylum Seekers," by Desmond Fernandes, a report available from Peace in Kurdistan, London, 2001, in *Variant*, 2,14 (Winter 2001) <variant.org.uk/14texts/14text>. Fernandes writes: "They will try and infiltrate the group and get a feel for the group and . . . they will often use inducements. They will say 'We will give you the right to stay in this country. We will get you a passport, if you give us information, if you will inform on your group.'"

3. Allan Thompson, "Not Our Policy to Coerce Refugees, CSIS Director Says," *The Toronto Star*, May 1, 1998.

4. Allan Thompson, "Minister to Seek Probe of Spy Agency," *The Toronto Star*, April 30, 1998, p. A 26.

5. David H. Martin, "The Candu Syndrome: Canada's Bid to Export Nuclear Reactors to Turkey," Campaign for Nuclear Phaseout report, September 1997, section 8.6 <http://www.ccnr.org/turkey_syndrome.html>.

6. Richard Sanders, "Arms Sales Support Turkey's War against the Kurds," *Peace and Environment News*, May 1995 <http://www.perc.ca/PEN/1995-05/sanders>.

7. A similar and more powerful dynamic was taking place in the U.S. Congress. At the time both the United States and Israel refused to recognize the genocide—specifically because of trade and military considerations. President Bill Clinton intervened, saying, "We have significant interests in this troubled region of the world. Consideration of the resolution at this sensitive time will negatively affect those interests." CNN.com, "U.S. House Shelves Armenia Genocide Bill: Legislation Sparked Protests by Turkish Government, Citizens," Oct. 19, 2000. See also <http://archives.cnn.com/2001/WORLD/europe/02/10/turkey.genocide/index>.

8. "Security Certificates," Public Safety Canada <http://www.publicsafety.gc.ca/prg/ns/seccert-eng.aspx>.

CHAPTER 6: THE NAMELESS ONE

1. In writing this book I have respected the secrecy provisions of the SIRC complaint process. However, I have made reference to several documents that are now public: 1) Report of the Security and Intelligence Review Committee, Feb. 17, 2000; 2) documents obtained through Access to Information and Privacy requests by Suleyman Goven and Andrew Brouwer (Brouwer's request for information was made on Feb. 27, 2007, and the documents were received in January 2010; by law these requests must be responded to within thirty to sixty days); 3) materials submitted in a Federal Court of Canada case, *Goven v. Canada (Minister of Citizenship and Immigration)*, 2002 FCT 1161, (2002), [2003] 3 F.C. D-3, Docket IMM-1740-01; decision rendered Nov. 12, 2002.

2. Herman Ebbinghaus, *Memory: A Contribution to Experimental Psychology* (New York: Teachers College, Columbia University, 1913). This is considered the standard work on memory as it fades over time.

3. Quoted from the transcript of the hearings. In a letter to me of April 10, 2001, Susan Pollack, Executive Director of the Security Intelligence Review Committee, concluded that SIRC could not investigate the forgery because the notice had been generated by Canada Immigration, not CSIS. There is no watchdog body to oversee Canada Immigration.

4. Stewart Bell and Marina Jiménez, *National Post*, May 11, 2000. (This article and the article cited in note 5 were found in CSIS files obtained through an Access to Information request; no titles were given.)

5. Stewart Bell, *National Post*, July 3, 2000.

6. "CSIS Comments on the Report of the Security Intelligence Review Committee, February 17, 2000, into the Complaint of Suleyman Goven Pursuant to Section 41 of the Canadian Security Intelligence Service Act." Document obtained through an Access to Information Act request.

7. The Hon. Elinor Caplan, former Minister of Immigration, as told to June Callwood, March 2005. Caplan was Minister of Immigration during the period following the SIRC recommendation. Following the implementation of the Immigration and Refugee Protection Act in 2002, responsibility for immigration security was transferred to the new Canada Border Services Agency.

8. Anne Dello is the only government official who can be named in this story, and that is because her "Decision and Reasons" (March 20, 2001) were entered as evidence in the Federal Court Application for Judicial Review (Court File: IMM-1740-01) and are thus a matter of public record. All the other officials remain nameless.

9. Citizenship and Immigration Canada, Field Operation Support System (FOSS) database, Ottawa, file no. 2684-2288.

10. Federal Court of Canada, *Goven v. Canada (Minister of Citizenship and Immigration)*, 2002 FCT 1161, (2002), [2003] 3 F.C. D-3, Docket IMM-1740-01; decision rendered Nov. 12, 2002.

11. Although Amnesty International, *Annual Report 2009*, indicates that the PKK still operates an armed struggle for Turkey. See chapter 3, n.3.

12. See Office of the Auditor General of Canada, *2004 March Report*, section 3.114, Ottawa. The 2009 *March Status Report of the Auditor General*, which reviewed compliance with recommendations made in 2004, indicated that the reliability of watch lists remained "unsatisfactory."

CHAPTER 7: THE BREAK OF DAY

1. Rather than serve and file a statement of defence, the government brought a motion to strike down Suleyman Goven's civil suit in January 2006. The hearing of the motion began in April 2006 at the Federal Court on University Avenue, with another sitting in May. The lawsuit was not dropped even after Suleyman finally got landed status on Sept. 7, 2006. The hearing on the government's strike motion continued in October 2006 and February 2007. By that time a similar civil suit (that of Nawal Haj Khalil) had been scheduled for trial, and the lawyers held Suleyman's case in abeyance while the Federal Court considered the other case and made a decision. Haj Khalil lost her civil suit at first instance and later also lost in the Court of Appeal. As of May 2010 the case was on its way to the Supreme Court of Canada. In the meantime Suleyman Goven's civil suit continued to be held in abeyance, pending a decision from the Supreme Court of Canada.

2. Canada's continuing close relationship with Turkey is evident on the website of the Government of Canada, under the heading "Canada-Turkey Relations": "In recent years, as friends and allies, Canada and Turkey have expanded the depth and variety of their bilateral links as valued political, commercial, strategic, and security partners" <http://www.canadainter national.gc.ca/turkey-turquie/bilateral_relations>.

3. Press release, Armenian National Committee of Canada, Ottawa, April 22, 2004.

APPENDIX A

1. O. Elagab, *International Law Documents Relating to Terrorism*, 2nd ed. (London: Cavendish Publishing Limited, 1997), p.xx; T.H. Mitchell, "Defining

the Problem," in D.A. Charters, ed., *Democratic Responses to International Terrorism* (New York: Transnational Publishers, 1991), pp.10, 11. The words terrorism and terrorist are placed within quotation marks throughout this article in recognition of their meaninglessness as a legal category.

2. CSIS, "Trends in Terrorism," Report #2000/01, 18 Dec. 1999 <www.csis. gc.ca/eng/miscdocs/200001e.html>, p.2; and *Report of the Special Senate Committee on Security and Intelligence* (Kelly Committee), January 1999 <www.parl.gc.ca/36/1/parlbus/commb.../com-e/secu-e/rep-e/repsecint jan99-ehtm> c.1, p.2.

3. Kelly Committee, c.1, p.14.

4. B. Gorlick, "The Exclusion of 'Security Risks' as a Form of Immigration Control: Law and Process in Canada" (1991), 5:3 *Immigration and Nationality Law and Practice*, p.76.

5. See P. Shah, "Taking the 'Political' out of Asylum: The Legal Containment of Refugees' Political Activism" in F. Nicholson and P. Twomey, eds., *Refugee Rights and Realities* (Cambridge: Cambridge University Press, 1999), pp.119-35.

6. R. Whitaker, "Refugees: The Security Dimension" (1998), 2:3 *Citizenship Studies* 413, pp.427, 430. Institutional racism can manifest itself in the form of explicitly racist policies in which the state directly reinforces racist biases in society, or it can be found in systemic form ("systemic racism"), concealed in systems, practices, policies, and laws that appear to be neutral and universalistic, but disadvantage racialized persons.

7. Canadian Council for Refugees, *Report on Systemic Racism and Discrimination in Canadian Refugee and Immigration Policies*, in preparation for the U.N. World Conference on Racism, Racial Discrimination, Xenophobia and Related Intolerance, 1 Nov. 2000 <www.web.net/~ccr/antiracrep.htm>.

8. H. Bannerji, *The Dark Side of the Nation* (Toronto: Canadian Scholars' Press, 2000), p.115. See also D. Matas, "Racism in Canadian Immigration Policy," in C. James, ed., *Perspectives on Racism and the Human Services Sector* (Toronto: University of Toronto Press, 1996); L. Jakubowski, "Managing Canadian Immigration: Racism, Ethnic Selectivity, and the Law" in E. Comack et al., *Locating Law, Race/Class/Gender Connections* (Halifax: Fernwood Publishing, 1999); A. Simmons, "Racism and Immigration Policy,"

in V. Satzewitch, ed., *Racism and Social Equality in Canada* (Toronto: Thompson Educational Publishing, 1998).

9. For an excellent account of one such interview/interrogation as experienced by Suleyman Goven, a Kurdish refugee from Turkey, see M.J. Leddy, *At the Border Called Hope* (New York: Harper Collins, 1997), pp.76-82; and the conclusions of the Security Intelligence Review Committee (SIRC), "In the Matter of the Complaints under the Canadian Security Intelligence Service Act by S.G. and S.D.," SIRC File, No. 1500-82, 83,7 April 2000, in which the Committee upheld two complaints, recommending in particular the need for Canadian Security Intelligence Service (CSIS) officials who are making assessments to develop a more sophisticated analytic framework, and the entitlement of the applicant to written notice of the date and time of the interview, its purpose, and the fact that the applicant has the right to attend with counsel (p.31). Goven's complaint was one of three immigration security screening complaints on which SIRC rendered decisions in 2000. In the wake of SIRC's findings in these three cases, a new policy was adopted that would provide applicants two to eight weeks' written notice of the interview by a convocation letter specifying that the interview will be with a CSIS employee. See *SIRC Annual Report, 1999-2000* p.82, footnote 33 <www.sirc-csara.gc.ca/annual/1999-2000/ar9900_e.html>.

10. J.J. Paust et al., "Terrorism," in *International Criminal Law: Cases and Materials*, 2nd ed. (Durham, N.C.: Carolina Academic Press, 2000), pp.999-1000.

11. See P. St. John, "Counterterrorism Policy Making: The Case of Aircraft Hijacking, 1968-1988," in D.A. Charters, ed., *Democratic Responses to International Terrorism*, pp.73-77.

12. N.J. Schrijver, "Interpreting the Principles and Purposes of the United Nations," in P.J. van Krieken, ed., *Refugee Law in Context: The Exclusion Clause* (The Hague: T.M.C. Asser Press, 1999), pp.237, 244. See also *Reference Re Secession of Québec* [1998] 2 S.C.R. 217.

13. R. Higgins, "The General International Law of Terrorism," in R. Higgins and M. Flory, eds., *Terrorism and International Law* (London: Routledge, 1997), p.16.

14. In all 120 states voted in favour of the establishment of the ICC, and 22 of the 60 states required for the Statute to enter into force have ratified it.

Canada signed the Rome Statute in December 1998 and ratified it 7 July 2000. See <www.un.org/law/icc/statute/status/htm>. The Rome Statute is the most current codification of a universal approach to combating serious international crimes. See <www.un.org/law/icc/statute/romefra.htm>. Within the ambit of "war crimes," defined in Article 8, are wilful killing, torture, taking of hostages, intentionally directing attacks at civilian populations or civilian objects, and attacking or bombarding undefended towns or buildings. The Statute sets a higher threshold for crimes committed in internal wars, stating that the Court's jurisdiction extends only to acts that take place in a state in which there is a "protracted armed conflict between government authorities and organized armed groups or between such groups." See Rome Statute, art. 25(3), "Individual Criminal Responsibility," art. 28, "Responsibility of Commanders and Other Superiors," and art. 30, "Mental Element."

15. P. Webster and I. Brodie, "G7 Vow to Pursue Terrorists," *The Times*, 27 June 1996, p.14. Ironically, the United States has refused to sign the 1998 Convention for the Suppression of Terrorist Bombings.

16. Criminal Code, ss. 76, 77, 78, 78.1.

17. J.J. Paust et al., "Terrorism," note 19, p.1020.

18. A.P. Schmid and A.J. Jongman, *Political Terrorism: A New Guide to Actors, Concepts, Data Bases, Theories and Literature* (New Brunswick, N.J.: Transaction Books, 1988), pp.1-38; J.F. Murphy, "The Need for International Cooperation in Combatting Terrorism" (1990), 13 *Terrorism: An Int'l. J*, 381, *quoting* W. Lacqueuer (citation omitted). On the lack of definition, see R. Slater and M. Stohl, "Introduction," in R. Slater and M. Stohl, eds., *Current Perspectives in International Terrorism* (New York: Macmillan, 1988), pp.1-11; A.P. Schmid and R.D. Creliston, *Western Responses to Terrorism* (London: Frank Cass, 1993), p.11; and P.P. Heymann, *Terrorism and America* (Cambridge: MIT Press, 1998), pp.3-9.

19. J. Lambert, "The Problem of International Terrorism and the Response of International Organizations," in P.J. van Krieken, *Refugee Law in Context: The Exclusion Clause* (The Hague: T.M.C. Asser Press, 1999), p.177; W. Lacqueur, ed., *The Terrorism Reader* (1979), p.262, and ———, *The Age of Terrorism* (1987), p.11, as cited in J. Lambert, "The Problem of International Terrorism and the Response of International Organizations," in van

Krieken, *Refugee Law in Context*, p.177; G. Levitt, "Is 'Terrorism' Worth Defining?" (1986), 13 *Ohio N.U.L. Rev.* 97; R. Higgins, "General International Law of Terrorism," p.28; J. Borricand, "France's Responses to Terrorism," in R. Higgins and M. Flory, eds., *Terrorism and International Law*, p.145.

20. J. Zulaika and W. Douglas, *Terror and Taboo* (New York: Routledge, 1996), pp.96-99.

21. N. Chomsky, *Necessary Illusions: Thought Control in Democratic Societies* (Concord, Ont.: House of Anansi Press, 1991), p.287; and see ——, *The Culture of Terrorism* (London: Pluto Press, 1988); ——, *Pirates and Emperors* (Toronto: Between the Lines, 1991). In a similar critique, Said notes that the terms fundamentalism and terrorism "signify moral power and approval for whoever uses them, moral defensiveness and criminalisation for whomever they designate." E. Said, *Culture and Imperialism* (London: Chatto and Windus, 1993), p.375.

22. E. Herman and G. O'Sullivan, *The Terrorism Industry: The Experts and Institutions That Shape Our View of Terror* (New York: Pantheon Books, 1990), pp.218-19.

23. R. Falk, *Revolutionaries and Functionaries: The Dual Face of Terrorism* (New York: E.P. Dutton, 1988), p.164.

24. "Colombo Hails Ban on the LTTE," *The Hindustan Times*, 10 Oct. 1997. A few months later, in January 1998, the Sri Lankan government formally outlawed the LTTE.

25. E. Chadwick, *Self-Determination, Terrorism and the International Humanitarian Law of Armed Conflict* (The Hague: Martinus Nijhoff Publishers, 1996), p.120.

26. Ibid., p.3.

27. Wilkinson suggests: "There should be no special privileges or discrimination in favour of those who plead political motives for their crimes of violence. According terrorists special status only serves to legitimise and perpetuate their own self-perception as 'freedom fighters.'" P. Wilkinson, "The Strategic Implications of Terrorism," in M.L. Sondhi, *Terrorism and Political Violence: A Sourcebook* (India: India Council of Social Science Research, Har-Anand Publications, 2000); and see ——, *Terrorism and the Liberal State*, 2nd ed. (London: Macmillan, 1986). For an analysis of the "terrorism industry," its links with Western governments, and the

scholarship that sustains it (including the work of Wilkinson), see Herman and O'Sullivan, *Terrorism Industry*.

28. None of the international instruments that identify the rights inhering in "peoples" actually define the term, thereby providing no guidance on which "peoples" are entitled to self-determination. In the early years of the U.N., states attempted to restrict the interpretation of the term in the interest of preserving territorial units. Scholars now suggest that the term "peoples" has evolved to mean groups that share common political goals, a will to live together, and clear ethnic and/or cultural ties. Chadwick, *Self-Determination*, pp.4-5.

29. International humanitarian law (IHL) includes two main branches: the law of war, and limited aspects of human rights law. It is principally concerned with *jus in bello*, that is, the rules applicable during armed conflicts, governing the conduct of hostilities and the protection of persons affected by the conflict. The primary treaty instruments that codify these rules are the four 1949 Geneva Conventions for the Protection of War Victims and the 1977 Protocols I and II Additional to the Geneva Conventions of 1949. The Geneva Conventions are considered customary, as are parts of the 1977 Additional Protocols. International law also addresses *jus ad bellum*, that is, the rules governing resort to force. See A. McDonald, "Introduction to International Humanitarian Law and the Qualification of Armed Conflicts," in van Krieken, ed., *Refugee Law in Context*.

30. See *International Educational Development/Humanitarian Law Project*, Written Statement Submitted to the U.N. Commission on Human Rights, 53rd Session (1997), which addressed the question of the status of the LTTE in Sri Lanka.

31. C. Greenwood, *International Humanitarian Law (Laws of War): Revised Report for the Centennial Commemoration of the First Hague Peace Conference 1899*, May 1999, para. 3.10.

32. Whether a conflict is characterized as international or internal is relevant for two reasons. In an international conflict there is a right to armed resistance; there is also concomitant responsibility, as all violations of IHL will be subject to prosecution as universal jurisdiction offences. The traditional approach to the classification of conflict focuses on the technical status of the parties, while another approach has developed that focuses on the general

process of armed conflict and the presence of various "internationalizing" elements. Subject to some interpretive debate, an internal conflict becomes international when a "people" face conditions of colonialism, alien occupation, or racism, or the non-state party is recognized as a belligerent (either outside the state or by the established government), or a foreign state participates in the armed conflict. Many states will resist characterizing a liberation group as a "people" and their struggle as an "international" conflict because it represents an incursion on sovereignty. As Chadwick notes, a series of successful liberation wars has "led to alterations in common understanding regarding which 'Peoples' are entitled to assert claims for self-determination, and to use force to achieve their rights." Chadwick, *Self-Determination*, pp.4, 64.

33. As an expert witness in a Canadian immigration security case, Falk characterized the right of self-determination as "an emerging norm of customary international law that depends for its clarification and assessment upon the specific context within which the claim is being made." *Minister of Citizenship and Immigration and Solicitor General of Canada* v. *Suresh*, DES-3-95 (T.D.), Transcript vol. 48, 3 Feb. 1997, pp.33-34, 43-47.

34. Article 51 of the Charter of the United Nations, 1945, enshrines the "inherent right of individual and collective self-defence" in the face of armed attacks against member states of the United Nations.

35. *Geneva Conventions Act*, R.S.C. c. G-3, as am. S.C. 1990, c.14; Statement of the Canadian Delegation to the U.N. Commission on Human Rights, 21 Oct. 1996–1 Nov. 1996.

36. International Convention for the Suppression of the Financing of Terrorism, United Nations, 1999, art. 21.

37. W. Elcock, Submission to the Special Committee of the Senate on Security and Intelligence, 24 June 1998, p.11.

38. The government also has never initiated prosecutions of alleged torturers in the refugee population, despite the specific obligation to do so in the Convention against Torture and the Criminal Code. Denying safe haven through deportation continues to be the government's preferred strategy.

39. International Convention for the Suppression of the Financing of Terrorism, art.2.1, 2.5.

40. Ibid., art. 14. This limitation, known in extradition law as the "political offence exception," is also found in the European Terrorism Convention. For a discussion of the application of the political offence exception in the context of asylum and terrorism, see. J.C. Hathaway and C.J. Harvey, "Framing Refugee Protection in the New World Order" (2001) 34(2), *Cornell Int'l L.J.*

41. J.C. Hathaway, *The Law of Refugee Status* (Toronto: Butterworths, 1991), pp.176-79.

42. D. Stasiulus and N. Yuval-Davis, eds., *Unsettling Settler Societies: Articulations of Gender, Race, Ethnicity and Class* (London: Sage Publications, 1995), pp.23-24.

43. S.C. 1872, 35 Vict. Ch. 28, s.10; S.C. 1910, Edw. VII, ch. 27, s. 41, s. 23.

44. N. Kelly and M. Trebilcock, *The Making of the Mosaic: A History of Canadian Immigration Policy* (Toronto: University of Toronto Press, 1998), pp.181-82, 207-9. See also D.H. Avery, *"Dangerous Foreigners": European Immigrant Workers and Labour Radicalism in Canada, 1896-1932* (Toronto: McClelland & Stewart, 1979), p.87; and J. W. St. G. Walker, *"Race," Rights and the Law in the Supreme Court of Canada* (Canada: The Osgoode Society for Canadian Legal History and Wilfrid Laurier Press, 1997), p.250.

45. *Canada* v. *Dueck* (T.D.), T 938-95 (1998), n.144. A fascinating record of postwar immigration security procedures is contained in this Federal Court decision rejecting the government's application to revoke Dueck's citizenship.

46. R.S.C. 1952, ch. 325 and ss. 5 (l), 19 (a); S.C. 1966-67, ch. 90.

47. See A. Brannigan and Z. Lin, "'Where East Meets West': Police, Immigration and Public Order Crime in the Settlement of Canada from 1896 to 1940" (1999), 24 *Canadian Journal of Sociology* 87, p.91.

48. National policies on the admission and exclusion of foreigners are typically characterized as central aspects of state sovereignty. In this context, immigration has been characterized as a privilege rather than a right. See R. Plender, *International Migration Law*, 2nd ed. (Dordrecht, Netherlands: Martinus Nijhoff, 1988). By affording individuals the right to seek and enjoy asylum, the Refugee Convention represents a significant incursion on state sovereignty. However, neither the Convention nor other

international instruments impose an unequivocal obligation on states to admit or host refugees. This apparent contradiction is addressed in part through the application of *non-refoulement* provisions.

49. Whitaker, "Refugees," pp.419-20.

50. S.C. 1976-77, ch. 52.

51. Immigration Act, s. 19(1),(g).

52. Ibid., s. 19(l)(j).

53. See S. Aiken, "Racism and Canadian Refugee Policy" (1999), 18:4 *Refuge* 2.

54. Commission of Inquiry Concerning Certain Activities of the Royal Canadian Mounted Police, *Freedom and Security Under the Law, Second Report*, vol. 2 (Ottawa: Minister of Supply and Services Canada, 1981), pp.823; and vol. 1, pp.43-44.

55. Ibid., p.436.

56. Gorlick, "Exclusion of 'Security Risks,'" p.77.

57. CSIS Act, R.S. 1985, c. c-23, as am. by R.S., 1985 c.1 (4th Supp.). s. 2 (a), (b), (c), (d).

58. See, for example, Leddy, *At the Border Called Hope*; and SIRC, *Annual Report 1997-1998* (Ottawa: Minister of Supply and Services, 1998), pp.9-12.

59. SIRC File, No. 1500–82, 83.

60. *SIRC Annual Report 1999-2000*, Section 1, p.17.

61. See A. Thompson, "Not Our Policy to Coerce Refugees," *The Toronto Star*, 1 May 1998; "More Refugees Come Forward with Claims of CSIS Threats," *The Toronto Star*, 23 April 1998; "Spy Agency Tactic under Fire," *The Toronto Star*, 4 April 1998; "How a Spy Is Hired: Case of Tamil Refugee Claimant Shines Light on How CSIS Operates," *The Toronto Star*, 20 Jan. 1996. This has been difficult to "prove" for the purposes of formal complaints, as screening interviews are not taperecorded. Certain CSIS officers have been unable to recall such remarks when subsequently requested to address concerns on the manner in which an interview was conducted. Although complaints of this nature were raised in the cases of S.G. and S.D., the chair was unable to substantiate them with regard to the complainants themselves. The SIRC reports recommended that all security interviews should be recorded and retained until a decision on immigration status is determined by the Department

of Citizenship and Immigration. See SIRC File, No. 1500–83, p.32.

62. *Outlawing an Ancient Evil: Torture, Convention against Torture and Other Cruel, Inhuman or Degrading Treatment or Punishment, Initial Report of Canada* (Ottawa: Multiculturalism and Citizenship Canada, 1989), p.1.

63. *Re Singh and Minister of Employment and Immigration and 6 other appeals* [1985] 1 S.C.R. 177.

64. Immigration Act, s.38.1. See ss. 39-40.1 for details of the procedures.

65. Ibid., s. 19(1),(e),(iii), s. 19(1),(e),(iv),(C), s. 19(1),(f),(ii), (iii),(B).

66. Hon. D. Lewis, Solicitor General, *House of Commons Debates*, 132:163 p.12533, 22 June, 1992.

67. Immigration Act, s. 19 (1),(e),(iv),(A);(f),(iii),(A); s. 46.01(1),(e),(ii).

68. Note that s. 52 of the Immigration Act provides that persons subject to deportation may be allowed to leave "voluntarily" and to select the country to which he or she wishes to go, *unless* the Minister directs otherwise (emphasis added). A person who is not permitted to leave voluntarily will be removed to one of four destinations: (1) the country from which the person came to Canada; (2) the country in which the person last permanently resided before coming to Canada; (3) the country of which the person is a national or citizen; or (4) the country of that person's birth. If none of these countries is willing to receive the person, then the Minister may select any country willing to accept him or her. *With the approval of the Minister,* the person may select (within a reasonable period of time) any country willing to grant admission (emphasis added).

69. J. Shields, Parliamentary Secretary to the Minister of Employment and Immigration, *House of Commons Debates*, 132:163, 22 June 1992, pp.12504-5.

70. Interview with A. Brouwer, Maytree Foundation, 22 Nov. 2000. See also SIRC File, No. 1500-82, 83; and *SIRC Annual Report 1999-2000*.

71. The identification of a general principle of international law as *jus cogens* provides it with the status of "higher law," although disagreement exists on the precise scope and content of *jus cogens*. See Sir I. Sinclair, *The Vienna Convention on the Law of Treaties*, 2nd. ed. (Manchester: Manchester University Press, 1984), p.18.

72. EXCOM Conclusion No. 79 (XLVII), General Conclusion on International Protection (1996), para. (j).

73. In 1997 and 1998 Canada carried out deportations in contravention of requests from the Committee against Torture *(Tejinder Pal Singh v. Canada)* and the Inter-American Commission on Human Rights *(Roberto San Vicente v. Canada).* See Amnesty International, "Refugee Determination in Canada: The Responsibility to Safeguard Human Rights," Response to Government of Canada's White Paper, February 1999.

74. Bill C-31, The Immigration and Refugee Protection Act, ss. 30(1), (c), and (f). [The bill had not yet been implemented at the time this article was originally published—ed.]

75. See, for example, *The Report of the Special Senate Committee on Security and Intelligence,* Jan. 1999, ch. 2 p.11 <www.parl.gc.ca/36/1/parlbus/commb... /com-e/secu-e/repsecintjan99-ehtm>; Legislative Review Advisory Group, "Not Just Numbers, A Canadian Framework for Future Immigration," Recommendation 138; and the Security Intelligence Review Committee, *Annual Report 1997-1998,* Section 1 p.10 <www.sirc-csars.gc.ca/ar9798_ e.html>.

76. See Immigration Act, ss. 39.1, 39.2, and 40; also, s. 40.1.

77. "In Flux but Not in Crisis," *Report of the Special Committee on the Review of the CSIS Act and the Security Offences Act* (Ottawa: Queen's Printer, 1990); and see Gorlick, "Exclusion of 'Security Risks,'" p.79. In response to Bill C-31, SIRC expressed concern, noting its "unique expertise in acting as a competent tribunal to handle appeals related to intelligence and security matters—a capacity that Parliament intended it to have . . . this proposal would remove important existing safeguards in the activities of CSIS that could have a serious negative impact on national security, on individual rights, or on both." SIRC *Annual Report 1999-2000,* p.2.

78. Bill C-31, ss. 71, 72, 75, 108. For critical commentary see briefs submitted by UNHCR, *Comments on Bill C-31;* Canadian Council for Refugees; Maytree Foundation <www.web.net/~ccr>.

79. R. Romonow, J. Whyte, and L. Leeson, *Canada . . . Notwithstanding: The Making of the Constitution 1976-1982* (Toronto: Carswell/Methuen, 1984), p.218; M. Mandel, *The Charter of Rights and the Legalization of Politics in Canada* (Toronto: Thomson Educational Publishers, 1994), pp.68-74; and P. Russell, "The Political Purposes of the Canadian Charter of Rights and Freedoms" (1983), 61 *Can. Bar Rev.* 30, p.49.

APPENDIX B

1. When some of these Kurdish individuals do identify with their own ethnic origin, they suffer for it. In 1994 Turkey persecuted and later prosecuted fifteen members of Parliament who openly stated they were Kurds and voiced the demands of their own electorates—demands which the Turkish majority qualified as "terrorism," even though they were the demands of the people who had elected them.

2. The ERNK is trusted with a diplomatic peacetime mission and appears to be actively involved in international diplomacy, meetings with foreign governments and officials in an attempt to find a solution to the conflict through dialogue.

Acknowledgements

The Canada Council provided the financial resources that enabled me to write the first draft of this book at the Banff Centre for the Arts in Alberta. The Leighton Studios there was a helpful environment in which I could begin this story.

Writing this book forced me to draw on all my inner resources and on long and deep friendships. The Sanctuary Coalition in Toronto was a constant source of encouragement. Suleyman Goven and I owe all its faithful members a debt of gratitude. Michael Creal, the chairman of the coalition since its beginnings in the early 1990s, offered wise and welcome advice. His wife, Lee Davis Creal, went to extraordinary lengths to ensure publication of the manuscript. Her belief in the importance of this story is indicative of her own very deep commitment to justice.

Three lawyers grace the pages of this book as they struggled to secure justice for Suleyman Goven: Sharryn Aiken, Barbara Jackman, and Andrew Brouwer. They have done honour to their profession and given hope to us all. I am particularly grateful to Professor Aiken, who gave permission to reprint her fine article on the manufacturing of terrorists, which appears as Appendix A. The article is an excellent resource for those who want to pursue some of the implications of Suleyman's story.

A considerable amount of research went into laying the foundations for this book. Francesca Allodi-Ross, Jordan Poppenk, and Andrew Brouwer ensured that the story was constructed on a solid factual basis.

Finally, I want to thank Robert Clarke and the team of Between the Lines press. They have earned a justifiable reputation as a publisher of conscience and consequence. Rob's considerable editorial gifts have improved the original manuscript immensely.

Index

Group of 8 Ministerial Conference on
  Terrorism (1996), 150
Gulf War, first, 14, 21

"H." (rival of Suleyman's), 81, 106
Haj Khalil, Nawal, 184n1(ch.7)
Halkin Kurtuluşu (People's Liberation),
  63
Harper, Stephen, 142
Hathaway, J.C., 158
Heaven's Gate and Hell's Flames, 23
Herman, E., 152
Higgins, R., 148, 151
hijacking, 147
Hitler, Adolf, 51
Hošek, Chaviva, 119
human rights: Canada's compliance
  with international standards, 164;
  security and, 171; trade vs. 90–91,
  133; violations of, 155
Human Rights Association of Turkey, 18
Human Rights Watch, 176
Hungary, 162

Ignatieff, Michael, 142
immigrants: perceived threat of terrorism by, 144–47; vetting of, 160–74;
  visa requirements for, 160
Immigration Canada, 13, 87; accountability of, 122–23; class action suit
  and, 130; disregarding of SIRC
  recommendations by, 117–19, 121,
  129; dissatisfaction with, 88; recommendation by CSIS sent to, 80; relationship of with CSIS, 116–17;
  Suleyman's security interviews at,
  35–36, 37–43, 77–78, 82, 88, 102–5,
  109, 117–18

Immigration intelligence, lack of watchdog for, 122
immigration law and policy, 144–47;
  admissibility provisions of, 165–66,
  168, 169, 172, 174; national security
  and, 159–74. *See also* Canada
Immigration Security, 116–17
immigration security policy, 144–47,
  161, 164–65
Inan, Hüseyin, 56
India, 147
Inter-American Commission on
  Human Rights, 171
"international crimes," 149
International Criminal Court (ICC), 149;
  Rome Statute, 149
international law, 154–55, 170–71;
  humanitarian, 149, 156
International Monetary Fund (IMF), 59
"international terrorism," definitions
  of, 151
Iran: collapse of Shah's regime in, 62;
  Kurds from, 25, 52, 176
Iraq: Kurds from, 14, 21, 25, 26, 176;
  war in, 133
Irish Republican Army (IRA), 40
Islam, 12
Israel: Armenian genocide and, 182n7;
  description of Palestinian conflict,
  144; hijacking of aircraft from, 147
Italy, belonging to terrorist
  organization as crime in, 150
Izady, Mehrdad R., 53

Jackman, Barbara, 97, 103, 107, 121,
  130
Jamie Mosque, 11–12
Jordan, hijacking of aircraft from, 147

Mary Jo Leddy is a writer, speaker, theologian, and social activist. An Adjunct Professor at Regis College and Senior Fellow at Massey College, both at the University of Toronto, she is also the founder and director of Romero House in Toronto and a member of the Order of Canada. Her previous books include *Radical Gratitude* and *At the Border Called Hope: Where Refugees are Neighbours*.